HICKORY
FURNITURE

HICKORY
FURNITURE

Written and photographed by Ralph Kylloe

GIBBS SMITH

Gibbs Smith, Publisher
Salt Lake City

For my daughter, Lindsey, the thrill of my life! May she
love rustic furniture as much as I do.

First Edition
10 09 08 07 06   5 4 3 2 1

Text © 1995, 2006 Ralph Kylloe
Photographs © 2006 Ralph Kylloe

Published by
Gibbs Smith, Publisher
P.O. Box 667
Layton, Utah 84041

Orders: 1.800.835.4993
www.gibbs-smith.com

Designed by Rudy Ramos
Printed and bound in Hong Kong

Library of Congress Cataloging-in-Publication Data

Kylloe, Ralph R.
  Hickory furniture / Ralph Kylloe.   1st ed.
    p. cm.
  Includes bibliographical references.
  ISBN 1-58685-809-2
  1. Country furniture—Indiana. 2. Hickory furniture—Indiana.
I. Title.

NK2435.I5K95 2006
749'.1—dc22

2006010483

CONTENTS

INTRODUCTION

Around 1978 I was a doctoral student at Boston University. My housemate at that time was John Ames, an antiques dealer. One day he brought home a massive oval dining room table. It had log legs that retained their original bark. The table was signed Old Hickory Chair Company, Martinsville, Indiana. I fell in love with the table and with my last dollar purchased it from my friend for $280. Two months later he purchased the table back from me for $400. I was thrilled with the $120 profit and even more thrilled with the realization that hickory furniture actually did exist. I was hooked and spent the next few years learning the antiques business.

I wrote my first book on hickory furniture in 1988. Its title was Indiana Hickory Furniture. It was just a small stapled booklet with a bit of history and reprints of a few early hickory furniture catalogues. I printed five hundred copies and they sold out in a month. I then came out with another book titled Indiana Hickory Furniture Makers in 1989. It was another inexpensive book but I had done more research and offered a further history on the hickory furniture movement for that book. It took a year to sell fifteen hundred copies.

A year later I spoke before the annual Arts and Crafts Conference in Asheville, North Carolina, about rustic furniture and about the Indiana Hickory Furniture movement. I also had a booth at their antiques show and offered several examples of hickory furniture for sale. All of my furniture sold almost immediately. I was thrilled.

It was at that conference that I met Dr. Robert M. Taylor of the Indiana Historical Society. He loved the furniture and my meager attempts to document the history of the movement. He encouraged me to apply for a grant from the State of Indiana, which I did.

A few years later I was awarded a CLIO grant from the Indiana Historical Society. The CLIO grant is a literary award given to individuals who have researched and preserved the rich history of Indiana. In 1995 I published A History of the Old Hickory Chair Company and the Indiana Hickory Furniture Movement. The title was probably too long, but I sold out the first edition of

These early hickory chairs characterized by pointed posts and often a swirled brass tack topping the leg date from the early 1900s. Chairs at that time were woven with thin strips of hickory. Such chairs are pictured in the 1901 Old Hickory Chair Company catalogue. This collection resides in Martinsville, Indiana.

2,500 in about two years. I expanded the book in 2002 to include the 1901 Old Hickory Chair Company catalogue (which, by the way, cost me nearly $800 on eBay!). At this writing, the five thousand copies of the second edition are nearly sold out.

At the conclusion of that book, I commented on the continuing interest in hickory furniture. In truth, although factory-made, hickory furniture is a great American folk art. It has withstood the test of time. It's honest stuff and built to last for ages. Its popularity continues to grow. Today there are three major companies building hickory furniture and several other small start-up companies that are also producing hickory products.

Old Hickory Furniture was relocated to Shelbyville, Indiana, and opened its doors in the early 1980s. Short-lived, the company was sold after just a few years. It was then run by Craig Campbell and Chris Williams. Tragically, Campbell passed away and Chris Williams, who briefly ran the company, left the firm. Today Old Hickory is thriving and has about 120 employees. They ship their furniture to every state in the nation and to numerous countries around the world.

A few years after the opening of Old Hickory, Flat Rock Furniture, Inc., opened its doors. Offering different styling, Flat Rock has captured a share of the market with innovative designs. A third company, Appalachian Rustic Furnishings, opened its doors in Georgia. Offering an assortment of products, they, too, have national presence.

Several small start-up firms around the state of Indiana also offer hickory furniture. A few of these companies are listed in the resource section of this book.

On another point, I am always amazed at how information on hickory gets confused. It seems that just about anything with bark on it is erroneously called Old Hickory furniture by the general public. An example of this can clearly be seen on eBay. Under the category of Old Hickory, you'll find all kinds of stuff called Old Hickory that, in truth, is really something else. An absolute rule of thumb is that if its not signed Old Hickory, then it is not Old Hickory. Keep in mind that there were ten different companies building hickory furniture and very few of them actually signed their pieces.

So another reason for the publication of this book is to educate those with interest in hickory furniture as well as to document the history and the on-going evolution of the rustic movement here in North America. It is a movement that is rooted in the culture of all humanity. Hickory furniture is folk art at its finest.

BEGINNINGS OF HICKORY FURNITURE MANUFACTURE

No one really knows who built the first rustic chair out of hickory wood. But probably some individual hunter passing through Indiana ten thousand years ago rolled a hickory log in front of a fire, sat down on it to watch the evening's catch cook, and there was the first hickory chair.

Several thousand years passed and newspapers began printing and recording the daily happenings of the human race. Many important things were written about, and once in a long while someone would write something about an obscure individual who was doing something almost totally unnoticed by the rest of humanity. Such is the case with individuals who built rustic furniture.

From the start I should mention that there are conflicting reports regarding the beginnings of the Indiana hickory furniture movement. It should also be mentioned that many of the bits and pieces of information I have acquired and present here came to me as articles torn from very early newspapers that were not dated. Some articles, I believe, came from the late 1800s and provided very interesting information, but not documentable proof, that something actually happened. Other articles were dated and offered a compelling glance at the beginnings of the hickory furniture movement.

Most of this early information came from the Morgan County Library historical archives, the Morgan County Recorder of Deeds, the State of Indiana Department of Corporations and libraries from the surrounding communities as well. However, once the various companies incorporated, the trail was significantly easier to follow.

One undated article that is most compelling states that hickory furniture "had its conception in the mind of an ingenious fellow named Burch at Monrovia along about 1880. There he made, in a crude way, chairs from hickory, bending the poles from manpower and stripping the bark for weaving with

This early porch swing provides ample opportunity for relaxing moments. Woven in traditional herringbone pattern with with hickory strips, the piece was made by the Old Hickory company of Martinsville.

a pocket knife. The chairs were not only novel but substantial, and people bought them. Two or three others became associated in the business and as the 'plant' branched out, one hustling young man rented the old abandoned Christian Church on Pike Street in Martinsville and started a factory. This was a one-person concern for some time under the control of an 'immigrant' from Tennessee."

There is no official record of a man named Burch in the Monrovia archives, but it is very possible that the "immigrant" referred to in the article was Edmond L. Brown of Martinsville. (Early documents, including his own signature, indicate that his name was Edwin; later he is listed in documents as Edmond.)

But other evidence and other players existed as well.

Mr. James Wisby, local historian extraordinaire from Morgantown, mentions that there were two or three individuals building hickory hoop chairs in barnyards in Morgantown just prior to the turn of the century. To date, two very distinct styles of hickory chairs have emerged and both were from Morgantown.

Individuals have mentioned that Mr. Billy Richardson of Morgantown made hickory chairs at the turn of the century. Richardson was originally a lumberman and gardener who made a living out of his wagon with rustic hoop chairs. It took Richardson a full day to construct one hoop chair and a little longer for settees and tables. He sold them on the weekends from a horse-drawn wagon in the square at Martinsville, only a few miles down the road from Morgantown. According to his granddaughter Erma Lory, Billy Richardson was "good old-fashioned people. Good Christian people," she said proudly of her grandfather. He had "a long beard and was really nice and a very hard worker," she said. He had two brothers, Howard and Wilbur, and five kids: James, Deli, Mary, Nola and Cory.

His chairs are easy to identify because they are unique. His chairs are quite primitive looking, and the mortises are cut completely through the legs. The finials are all pointed and all the joints are cut completely through the posts. Family members still have a few chairs of his and one individual has collected several Billy Richardson chairs over the years.

It is obvious that at least one other individual was creating hickory hoop chairs in Morgantown. A collection of at least ten Morgantown chairs exists, and it is apparent from examination that the chairs are from two different builders. One style is clearly from Richardson while the other group is not as pointed at the ends and has a tendency to be smaller. No other names have surfaced to which the chairs can be attributed.

It is also interesting to note that the following was reported in 1949 in *Business and Industry Magazine:* "The first chairs made near Morgantown were made by Mr. Richards who lived at Morgantown and he made chair #32 which is the original Andrew Jackson chair and which has become the trade mark of the company. He is said to have made thirty chairs a year."

Another undated early article states that "Mr. A. Richards of Morgantown made the first chairs. They were like #32 in the catalogue. He had learned his art in the mountains of North Carolina. As a boy, he had helped his father make a set of chairs for Andrew Jackson."

The Mr. Richards referred to in these articles is probably Billy Richardson of Morgantown.

Another untitled and undated, but old, article states the following about the beginnings of the hickory business: "The first company 1892, consisted of M. B. Crist of Indianapolis and George Richardson. They made four styles of chairs in the old Christian Church, now the laundry. In 1895, the factory was sold to William F. Churchman, L. E. Brown." Although the article refers to L. E. Brown, the correct name is Edmond L. Brown.

Another compelling article written in 1949 by a longtime Martinsville resident concurs with the above and offers more information on the subject. The author begins her article with the very definitive:

This much we know for fact. Mr. M. B. Crist of Indianapolis in passing through Morgantown saw one of the chairs at an old hotel. He carried it home by way of Martinsville and there he met George Richards who later formed a partnership with Mr. Crist and started the factory in the Old Christian Church on Pike Street now occupied by the Artesian Laundry. . . . William Churchman and E. L. Brown bought the plant in 1895. The Shireman Brothers, Mr. E. C. and Mr. Max Shireman purchased a share in the business a short time after this and later bought out the factory.

A different newspaper article, also undated but very old, paints a different picture. In discussing the beginnings of the company, they offer that in 1898 the owners of the company were F. W. Wood, president and also owner of the

Facing: This contemporary drop-leaf table is from the Flat Rock Hickory Furniture Company. The hanging wall shelf from the Old Hickory Furniture Company was probably created in the 1940s.

Right: Both the tea cart and the high chair appeared in the 1931 Old Hickory catalogue. Both pieces are very rare. My daughter grew up in the high chair and succeeded in spilling more Cheerios, pancakes and milk on the chair than I care to remember!

Below: This bureau was created in the 1920s by the Rustic Hickory Furniture Company of Laporte, Indiana. It was the only company to offer spindles below the mirror. The table lamp is from the Old Hickory company. Both the antler floor lamp and the table lamp have antique mica shades.

Facing: A bookcase rests in the hallway. Extra spindles, reflecting the Arts and Crafts period from the early part of the twentieth century, add depth to the design.

A spindle umbrella stand and diminutive bookcase occupy the living room of the cabin.

This rare desk and office chair provide a place for letter writing. The top of the desk is solid oak and the chair both rocks and swivels. In 1914 the desk sold for $40 and the chair was offered for $16. Sitting next to the desk is a Keg Tabourette that originally sold for $3.

Woods-Goss Lumber Company; H. H. Woods, father of F. W. who was secretary of the firm and handled the front office; and E. L. Brown, superintendent.

But the one article that provides the clearest picture was published in the 1898 Industrial Edition of the *Martinsville Republican*. It reads that the

personnel of the company are Messers. F. W. Woods, president; H. H. Woods, secretary; and E. L. Brown, superintendent. Mr. F. W. Woods is a native of Michigan City and has been identified with the company for three years and is president of the Woods-Goss Lumber Company, of this city.

We then have two different articles that corroborate that the Woods family were the owners and that E. L. Brown was the superintendent.

Further, a catalogue printed in 1910 by the Old Hickory Chair Company states that early hickory chairs were "made at Martinsville, by an old craftsman

who had learned his art in the mountains of North Carolina. As a boy he had helped his father make a set of chairs for Andrew Jackson." They may well have been referring to Billy Richardson.

The plot thickens in another compelling article published in The Herald in 1976, by the Henry Ford Museum, which discusses the connection of Arts and Crafts designer Charles Limbert to the Indiana Hickory furniture movement. "He had seen handmade hickory chairs in Martinsville, Indiana, and discovered that they had been made for forty years by a Mr. Richardson, whose cousin George Richardson had started a factory near Martinsville for their production."

At any rate, the facts, according to what is available today, are presented above and the reader can only surmise that different individuals played different roles in the start of the company.

There is, however, temptation on the part of any author to make assumptions. Nonetheless, there is no definitive proof as to who actually started the Old Hickory Company. However, we do know that Billy Richardson of Morgantown produced hickory hoop chairs and sold them in Martinsville. At the same time, several documents state that an individual by the name of Richards/Richardson started the company. Unfortunately, neither the names of Richards or Richardson are listed in the genealogy records of that area. It may be safe to assume, however, that it was Billy Richardson who was the first individual to construct and market hickory chairs in Martinsville. He has been identified by several different family members and was well known in his time in the community. Further, a significant collection of his chairs exists and are known to be made by him. It is also interesting to note that a very early advertising piece from the Old Hickory Chair Company states the following:

> Many years ago, the organization that originated and first made this type of furniture, consisted of one man. He cut the poles in the fall and with the coming of spring, cut enough to weave them into chairs. They were then sold through the country from a wagon.

In reality, this sounds very similar to the business operation of Billy Richardson. Given this, he should receive credit for his efforts.

Facing above and this page: This dining room set, arguably the most impressive and complete set of early Old Hickory furniture presently known, rests in a seasonal lakeside cabin in the Adirondacks. The set has sat in the same place since 1926, when it was created for the camp. The round dining room table is expandable with a set of six leafs. The table has a top of solid oak and a very rare woven apron. The set of ten chairs includes both armchairs and side chairs.

Facing below left: A rare high chair with retractable tray provides seating for toddlers. Facing below right: This small serving table was custom made in 1926. This style of furniture first appeared in the 1914 Old Hickory catalogue. The table sold at that time for $50.

Above: This serving table stands 30 inches tall and is 42 inches long. As with most early Old Hickory pieces, the top is oak. The original price of the piece was $11.

Above right: This Old Hickory coat tree is usually hidden under mountains of sweatshirts, rain gear and jackets.

Right: This Old Hickory buffet is the only example of this piece ever found by the author. The buffet is six feet long and four feet high, with eleven drawers and two doors. Made of solid oak, the piece is nearly impossible to move. It was offered for $160 in 1914.

This set of chairs was custom made for the home. This very tall armchair with wrap-under seat never appeared in an Old Hickory catalogue. This sturdy set adds high drama to the setting.

This dining room set was constructed in the 1920s by the Rustic Hickory Furniture Company of Laporte, Indiana. Complete with four leafs and a set of ten chairs from the same company, the set often hosted my friends and family. The tabletop is oak. The armchairs sold originally for $13 each and the side chairs were $3.34 each. The floor lamp in the corner is Old Hickory, probably early 1940s. An antique mica shade rests on top of the lamp.

Facing: This setting is from a home I formerly owned in New Hampshire. As a long-time collector of hickory furniture, I can say that related items such as signs and advertising are highly sought after. The sideboard, chairs, table lamp and toy hickory pieces blend naturally in any rustic setting.

This set of huge armchairs sits outside the Lake McDonald
Lodge in Glacier National Park, Montana. Many national parks
purchased hundreds of pieces of hickory furniture, so it is not
uncommon for such parks to have lobbies full of hickory.

This mint-condition Old Hickory glider was probably constructed in the 1940s. Although Old Hickory gliders appeared earlier, a front piece of trim covering the front-seat weaving first appeared in the 1940s. The piece is woven with rattan in an "open weave" or "porch" pattern. Early gliders were fixed to the frame with chairs. Later gliders, such as the one shown, swung from the frame with ball-bearing metal supports.

Below: This breakfast set, made by the Rustic Hickory Furniture Company, sits on the porch of one of many cabins in Glacier National Park.

Facing: This chair and a few hundred just like it serve as seating for guests at the Old Faithful Inn in Yellowstone National Park. First appearing in the 1914 Old Hickory catalogue, the "Tavern Diner" chair sold for $3. The chairs have been in service at the inn for many decades. Because of their constant use, the park employs one individual to maintain the chairs by re-gluing and reweaving seats when necessary.

The dining room at the Old Faithful Inn is filled with a few hundred Old Hickory "Tavern Diner" side chairs.

This large contemporary panel bed is called a "Big Ranch" bed by the Old Hickory Furniture Company, presently in Shelbyville, Indiana.

Below left: This early hickory armchair was created in the Windsor style. The wooden plank seat is pine. The chair is unsigned and was probably made by a talented craftsman in the early twentieth century.

Facing below: On this traditional table lamp by the Old Hickory company, the grouping of hickory saplings is held together by copper bands. An antique mica shade sits on top of the lamp. The Old Hickory toy chairs were first featured in the 1901 Old Hickory catalogue. A boxed set of four pieces sold for $2. Many people confuse such pieces with salesmen's samples. Old Hickory never made salesmen's samples, and salesmen traveled with full-sized pieces when needed.

Right: This contemporary tall-case clock, table lamp and wing chair were made by the Old Hickory company. Part of the case front is covered with birchbark.

Left: The massive contemporary hall piece is called a "Big Ranch Buffet" by the Old Hickory company.

Right: This antique Old Hickory magazine stand presently houses part of my collection of fly-fishing rods. Antique creels and nets complete the setting.

Facing: A version of this very rare Old Hickory "Morris Chair" first appeared in their 1914 catalogue. It originally sold for $8.

My back porch contains this striking pair of early
chairs from the Old Hickory company. The extra
spindles reflect influence of the Arts and Crafts
movement. A variety of antique Adirondack items
adds to the setting.

This antique oval Old Hickory dining table is six feet long.
Complete with a solid oak top, the table comfortably seats
four. The "seven spindle" side chairs first appeared in the 1914
Old Hickory catalogue and sold for $2.50 each.

Right: These contemporary "Veranda Side Chairs" and round table were created by the Old Hickory company.

Below: The settee was constructed by the Indiana Willow Products Company, also of Martinsville, Indiana, in the 1940s. This company often used a product called Simonite, a by-product of spruce trees, as the weaving material for their seats and backs. In 1950, the company changed its name to the Indiana Hickory Products Company to reflect the fact that their furniture at that time was being constructed of hickory rather than willow.

Facing: Called the "Adirondack Chairs," these items first appeared in the 1941 Old Hickory catalogue. This fine pair of chairs rests in the Fisherman's Cabin at Manka's Inverness Lodge in Inverness, California. Filled with antique rustic accessories of all sorts, the room is a tribute to rustic design.

HICKORY
MANUFACTURERS

OLD HICKORY CHAIR COMPANY

All states have historical archives relating to the establishment of corporations within their state. Indiana has records for several of the other hickory furniture firms, but, unfortunately, the early records of the Old Hickory Chair Company—the largest and most prolific hickory company to have existed—had been destroyed by 1960, when records were being transferred to microfilm. Fortunately, the Morgan County Recorder of Deeds has maintained some files that shed light on the Old Hickory Chair Company.

MARTINSVILLE, INDIANA

Martinsville, Indiana, at the turn of the century, was a small community fortunately blessed with an entrepreneurial spirit. At that time, about twenty factories and mills existed in Martinsville, which included gristmills, lumberyards, tile businesses and others.

The possibility of natural gas and oil excited the state in 1887, and wells were drilled all over the state, including Martinsville. Unfortunately (or fortunately, depending on your perspective), neither gas nor oil was discovered in Martinsville. However, pure mineral water was found and in a short time Martinsville became known as Artesian City. "Around 1889, Captain Sylvan Barnard built a health sanitarium after mineral water was discovered . . . while drilling for gas at a depth of 550–650 feet" (the *Times*, 11–24, 1984). In a short period of time, thirteen health sanitariums existed in Martinsville, and people came from all over the country for mineral water baths.

Over a thousand rooms were available to visitors and many of these hotels had front porches that were filled with hickory chairs. It is interesting to note that the records indicate that "no hotel or mansion was complete without at least a dozen or so of these chairs scattered about their porches or lawns" (*Martinsville Republican*, Business and Industry, 1949).

The visitors to the sanitariums were very important to the establishment of the hickory furniture business as thousands of individuals were leaving Martinsville fully aware of the durability, comfort and beauty of hickory chairs.

The early years of the Old Hickory Chair Company were filled with what, in a business sense, can be referred to as wandering. Along with the four types of chairs they produced, the company also offered other intriguing products. Initially they offered riverboats for travel on the White River and fences made of hickory logs. They also offered complete log cabins for the price of $125 plus shipping. These products were soon dropped from their list of offerings as they quickly realized that they were selling many more chairs than riverboats.

BUILDING HICKORY FURNITURE

The construction of hickory furniture is not a complicated process. All items manufactured by the various companies were made by hand with simple tools. Initially, raw materials are acquired from the surrounding areas. The following elaborates on the process of gathering hickory trees.

86 Rocker

84 Drop Arm Readers' Chair

Old Hickory Chair Company, 1910.

No. 86 Rocker,
$11.25, height 42 inches, seat 22 inches wide,
17 inches deep.
No. 84 Drop Arm Readers' Chair,
$9.75.
No. 206 Table,
$8.25. Height 28 inches. Oak top,
16 inches square.
No. 212 Keg Tabourette,
$5.25. Height 18 inches, diameter 16 inches.
No. 226 Costumer,
$3.00. Height 5 feet 8 inches,
6 hooks.

206 Table

212 Keg Tabourette

226 Costumer

HICKORY POLE COLLECTING

On Friday, May 11, 1994, my wife and I spent the night at the Motel 6 on the outskirts of Indianapolis, just off Interstate 37. We drove south, turned left on Route 252 and drove into Morgantown. We went into the local cafe just down the street from what is probably the most historic and beautiful stone house in Indiana.

As we walked into the cafe, we were obviously given the once-over by the dozen or so locals who had probably spent many hours throughout their lives patronizing this local eating establishment. I had eaten there many times myself over the years and felt quite comfortable as we found a booth near the back of the restaurant. The waitress, whose personality was warm, open and friendly, was casual as she presented us with menus.

As we perused the offerings, my wife mentioned that the prices were a lot cheaper than in New York City. Neither of us was particularly hungry, so we ordered just a couple of cups of coffee. The bill for the coffee was twenty cents. We paid the check and left a dollar tip.

We had waited for the local hardware store to open and were now happy to see the lights on and people milling about.

We went into the back room and saw three elderly gentlemen sitting causally in comfortable wooden chairs that had been there for many years.

Being outgoing, my wife and I sat down in two empty chairs and commented that the hickory chairs that I had seen the last time I was in were no longer there. We did not move for the next three hours.

"Son, let me tell you about those chairs."

Harold Snider, seventy-nine years old and a lifelong resident of Morgan County, broke into a gracious smile as he began:

Old Hickory Chair Company, 1910. No. 312 Rustic Lawn Seat, Portable, $35. Width of each seat 18 inches. Length 42 inches.

Old Hickory Chair Company, 1910. No. 320 Summer House, $125. Size 10 feet square.

A stack of hickory poles at the Old Hickory company in Indiana. Poles are kiln dried and then sent through the manufacturing process.

"Back when I was fifteen years old I started cutting poles for the Old Hickory Company there in Martinsville. I had ten brothers and sisters. At that time we had no electricity, no phone and just an outhouse out back. Life was different then.

"Well, in the springtime, Old Hickory would advertise in the local paper for hickory poles. Now this was before autos so it wasn't easy. Well, they paid us ten cents a pole and they had to be straight with no branches or knots. They only bought the highest quality poles and would reject any that were not right.

"Most of the land that we collected poles on was owned by Brown County, but we often harvested on ours and other farms as well.

"We could collect about three hundred a day. We did this twice a week and it lasted for about two months in late winter only. Well, we cut the poles with either a two-person saw or a hand ax. We would trim the poles later. But we were very careful not to damage any of the young hickory trees because that was our bread and butter in years to come.

"Once we were through cutting and trimming the trees, we

Old Hickory Anniversary catalogue, 1931, No. 277 Desk. Top 36 x 22 inches overall, 30-1/4 inches from floor, shelves 17-1/2 x 6-1/2 inches, drawer 17 x 16-1/4 inches inside, floor to bottom of drawer 25-1/2 inches, envelope boxes 7-5/8 inches long, 2-1/2 inches wide, 3-1/2 inches deep inside. Dark oak finish.

Old Hickory Anniversary catalogue, 1931, No. 274 Stool. Size 10 x 16 inches, height 10 inches.

Old Hickory Anniversary catalogue, 1931, No. 35 Chaise Longue. Back 20 inches high; seat 57 inches long, 21 inches wide.

Old Hickory Anniversary catalogue, 1931, No. 5073 Bridge Lamp. Extreme height 58 inches, 2 light pull chains, fitted with imitation parchment shade 12 inches diameter.

Old Hickory Anniversary catalogue, 1931, No. 134 Couch. Length 82 inches, width 29 inches, woven top reinforced with coil springs under weaving.

loaded them onto a horse-drawn wagon pulled by two draught horses. We had to travel sixteen miles on dirt and gravel roads to deliver the poles. Many times the roads were icy or very wet and we had to put special shoes and pads on the feet of the horses to help them pull through the ice or mud.

"Once we were there, we delivered them to the receiving door. Workers at the plant helped us unload the poles. Once the poles were off the wagon, we would go to the office and get a check. They paid us the same day.

"Once in a while we would stop and play baseball at the park next to the plant with the other Old Hickory employees after they got out from work. They were very nice people at the Old Hickory Company. They were good to us and the whole business was good for the economy around the entire area. There were at least ten other men who cut poles for them in our area including Jake Baily, Walter Huron and a number of others.

"In 1941, I went into the army but started cutting poles for them again when I returned. I cut poles for them all the way until 1965 when they closed."

No. 301-SV Swing and Chains

No. 102-5 SV Settee

No. 242-SV Indian Seat

No. 1-SV Junior Glider

**Old Hickory Chair Company, 1931
Anniversary catalogue.**

No. 301-SV Swing and Chains
Length 4 feet, back 22 inches high; seat 20 inches deep.
No. 102-5-SV Settee
Back 22 inches high; seat 60 inches long, 20 inches deep.
No. 242-SV Indian Seat
Height 18 inches in center; top 14 x 24 inches.
No. 1-SV Junior Glider
Length overall 66 inches; back 21 inches high; seat 22 inches
deep. Furnished with and without canopy.
No. 22-SV Chair
Back 22 inches high; seat 17 inches wide, 20 inches deep.
No. 23-SV Rocker
Back 22 inches high; seat 17 inches wide, 20 inches deep.

No. 22-SV Chair

No. 23-SV Rocker

The eyes of Harold Snider seemed to shine as he recalled these earlier times. He was a tall man who was very bright and quick-witted. His two other friends bantered back and forth with him as he told his stories. They obviously had known each other for many years, and in between the stories of their efforts with Indiana hickory, they told of the storms, the battles, the fires, the weddings and divorces, the kids, and the many other tales that are forged in a lifetime.

As my wife and I said our good-byes, Harold Snider stood and broke into a big smile and roared with pride that Old Hickory . . . "built the best gall darn furniture you ever did see!"

THE BUILDING PROCESS

Second-growth hickory saplings that are cut in the winter when the sap is down, are used to make rustic hickory furniture. The bark will adhere to the wood if it is cut in winter. Cut in the spring, and the bark quickly loosens and falls away from the wood.

The wood is usually kiln dried and then chemically treated with insecticides to prevent infestation. One former employee of the Old Hickory plant mentioned that the chemicals were so toxic that "people definitely stayed out of the area where the chemicals were used."

The poles are then soaked in very hot water and bent into shape around sturdy steel forms. Once dried, the poles retain their new shapes and are sent to another area where they are drilled and formed into pieces of furniture.

In the early days of hickory furniture building, the wood from the hickory tree was stripped from the tree and rolled into long rolls weighing fifty pounds each. The rolls of bark were then boiled, sawn into strips, and then pulled through a leather splitter to acquire the desired thickness and uniformity. This material was then woven into the chairs as seats and backs. "Mr. Harrison Staley made the machine in his own shop which was used first for splitting the bark," reports *Business and Industry* magazine. It should be mentioned, however, that E. L. Brown held patents on a similar machine as well as other technology relating to the construction of hickory furniture.

As a rule, women did the weaving. "Women are more dependable," says Hugh Hines, manager of the Old Hickory plant in 1973. Other former managers reflected this sentiment.

On June 19, 1994, 1 was fortunate to speak with Dorothy Fletcher, whose mother, Cona Breedlove, was an employee at Old Hickory for fifteen years:

My mother was a real singer. She sang all day long and even when she went to work she always left singing. She worked at the plant for ten hours a day and she did that for fifteen years. She was a weaver and worked on the second floor with all the other girls. It was very hard work and I remember that her hands were always swollen and sore from pulling on the rattan that they used to weave the chairs. It was hard work but a very friendly place to work. All our friends worked there. It was a real family place and whenever a child was born it was announced over the loud speaker for everyone to hear. There was no air conditioning and it was very hot there in the summer but everyone got along real good.

Alice Burns, a woman with a great sense of humor and a twinkle in her eye, worked for the Old Hickory Furniture Company in Martinsville in the mid-1940s. She, like many other women of that time, was married at sixteen and began working at seventeen.

She went to work in the cabinet room at Old Hickory. Her job was to "rough up the furniture to make it look old," and she described the Old Hickory plant as a "very noisy place. It was very hard work and not at all glamorous," she said, and the "wages were very low. One nice thing about the company, however, was that the jobs were very secure. They never laid people off," she said. "It was a real family place—parents and sons and daughters both worked there and it was a very social place. On weekends there were picnics and baseball games. Most of the people who worked there had been there for many years, including Mary Neal, a legend at Old Hickory who had been there forever. Mary was the bookkeeper for the company and was the nicest lady," she commented.

The name of Mary Neal has surfaced many times, and it is known that when the Pattons, the company owners, were out of town, she had the company checkbook and was held responsible for feeding any kid in town who was hungry.

Alice mentioned that the weavers were artists, and she enjoyed watching them work. "Most of the people there worked on a quota system" and her boss, a man called Speedy, frequently told her to work faster. Alice found the work to be too difficult and she left her job after only two or three months.

"My husband, who worked in assembly, was so ashamed of me for quitting," she said.

THE ARTS AND CRAFTS CONNECTION

Proponents of the Arts and Crafts movement, specifically Gustav Stickley and Charles Limbert, sought simplicity and honesty in their work. They sought to keep things natural, unadorned and unencumbered. They did not try to deceive the viewers of their works by excessively manipulating the materials with which they worked.

This philosophy was consistent with the efforts of the craftsmen who made Indiana hickory furniture. The only difference between the two movements was that the Arts and Crafters were capable of articulating and expressing their ideologies and views toward their work and life in general. Rustic builders, on the other hand, being simple men and folk artists, were not and did not.

According to reports, Charles Limbert and probably Gustav Stickley both visited the health spas in Martinsville and saw the efforts of the hickory furniture builders.

An undated article from the *Herald* reports that Limbert "had seen hickory chairs in Martinsville" and persuaded a friend to buy the company. It is unclear exactly who that friend was, but, according to records, the owners at that time were the Wood Family from Indianapolis. Limbert, it was recorded, acted as agent for the company from 1896 to 1905. Limbert not only sold his own line of mission furniture but was a sales representative for at least five other companies as well.

He was so successful in his sales efforts that the Old Hickory company had difficulty in meeting demands for more furniture. One source mentions that the response from one ad created enough mail for Ed Brown to wallpaper his entire office from the envelopes of the orders.

Both Limbert and Stickley used hickory furniture in their

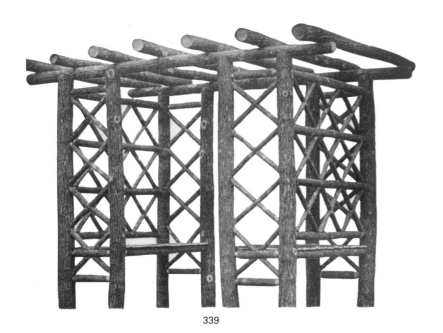

339

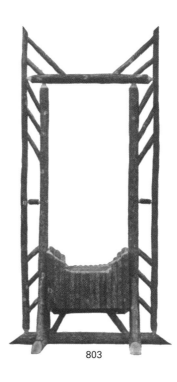

803

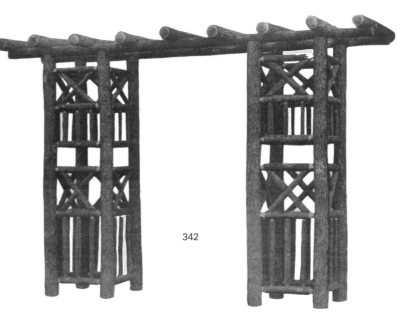

342

801

Old Hickory, Porch/Garden
catalogue, 1925

No. 339 Rustic Seat
Height 7-1/4 feet, width 8 feet,
seat 5 feet long.
No. 803 Flower Box Screen
Height 86 inches, length 42 inches.
No. 801 Rose Trellis
Height 100 inches, width
at top 5 feet.
No. 342 Rustic Entrance
Height 7 feet, width 8 feet.

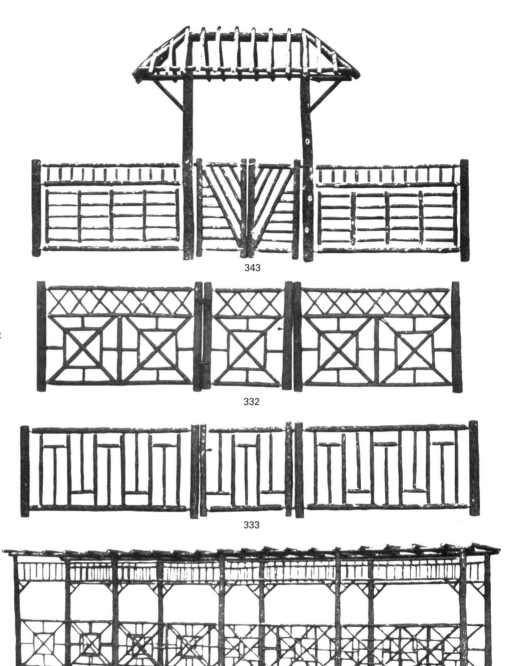

343

332

333

334

Old Hickory, Porch/Garden
catalogue, 1925

No. 343 Rustic Entrance
Complete with canopy, two 2-foot
gates and two 5-foot sections of
fence 44 inches high.
No. 332 Rustic Fence and Gate
Height 43 inches.
No. 333 Rustic Fence and Gate
Height 32 inches.
No. 334 Rustic Pergola
Height 8 feet, width 6 feet.

decorating projects. Many porches of Stickley's Craftsman Homes are pictured with hickory furniture, and photos show Limbert in his own home with hickory furnishings.

The Craftsman, March 14, 1914, describes hickory furniture as being "delightfully restful to the body" and maintaining a "simple dignity of design." In the same magazine in 1913, the writer declared that hickory furniture "has personality and a definite aire of sincerity." An early advertising piece from the Old Hickory company argues that their furniture "was put together with mortises as solidly as the best mission pieces" of the day.

There are striking similarities between pieces from the various hickory companies and the Arts and Crafts builders. Stickley presented his spindle series to the public in 1902, while Old Hickory showed pieces of hickory furniture heavily adorned with spindles in their 1900 catalogue. Old Hickory produced a wonderful Morris chair that had tight spindles under the arms that extended to the floor, which is similar to certain Morris chairs made by Stickley. Further, many tables, tabourets, settees, rockers, armchairs and side chairs made by Old Hickory are adorned with spindles and predate the works of Gustav and his brothers, who ran the often very similar L. & J. G. Stickley Company.

It is also interesting to compare the Prairie School efforts of Frank Lloyd Wright with pieces built by the hickory furniture makers. There are similarities. Take, for example, the #114 library table by the Rustic Hickory Furniture Company of Laporte. The table, heavily adorned with spindles, seems to have a rather profound Prairie School influence in that the varying layers of the desk seem to blend perfectly with many of Wright's tables and desks.

But the question remains: Did Old Hickory, in fact, invent the spindle series? The evidence seems to indicate just that, not to suggest that the Mission people did not carry the influence to new extremes. Nonetheless, Old Hickory and a parallel company, the Rustic Hickory Furniture Company of Laporte, Indiana, did produce stunning spindle pieces that predate the better-known and more respected Mission designers.

Limbert had been associated with the Old Hickory company since 1896, and Stickley knew of the company at that same time. There is great temptation on the part of experienced designers to suggest product design changes, especially to young companies that are not well established. It would have been very easy for Stickley, or at least Limbert, to offer suggestions on style and design.

One can be certain, however, that the two companies had a significant influence on each other. It is easily argued that mission furniture was far more popular than hickory furniture ever was. The facts are, however, that Old Hickory produced about two thousand pieces per week and they were in business for over sixty-five years.

The bottom line to the argument is that hickory furniture blends wonderfully with Mission and Prairie School furnishings. Their philosophies were identical. They both sought to be timeless and not subject to the whims of trends. They sought to blend with the environment. They both sought simplicity, comfort and a sense of naturalness. Both movements survived the ravages of age and are in the consciousness of people today because they met the criteria of the timelessness of art.

BRANCHING OUT

Records show that in 1895 the company was owned by the Wood Family and that E. L. Brown was the plant superintendent. Within a few years, the company was sold and the Wood Family returned to the lumber business.

Records further indicate that the company was owned in 1899 by Edmond L. Brown and Ralph Barret and was incorporated at that time. Brown, president, owned forty-nine shares and his wife, Lucy, owned one share. Ralph Barret also owned forty-nine shares and his wife, Gloria, owned one share. It was decided at the July 1900 board meeting to increase their capital stock to $20,000 and they looked for investors.

In July 1902, three new names were added to the list. Carl Nutter, W. A. Shireman and E. L. Shireman each had purchased seventy-five shares of the company. By the end of the month, Max Shireman also owned seventy-five shares and had been named the new company president, although Brown still owned one hundred shares.

At this time the Shiremans also owned a Morris chair factory. Brown left the Old Hickory Chair Company and purchased the Morris chair company from the Shiremans, and ran it for several years.

At the September 1, 1905, meeting, more shares were sold and J. W. Staub, W. C. Burke, Henry Lewis and W. R. McCracken each owned stock in the company. The three Shiremans owned 260 shares of the company between them.

In 1900, a new factory was completed at a cost of $6,000. At that time, the company was completing about seven hundred pieces a week. Within three months the output was doubled.

Max Shireman and his brothers owned and operated the business until 1908, when they decided that their hearts were in goldfish production. Martinsville was then the largest producer of goldfish in the world, and to this day a number of goldfish producers still reside there.

But the real shakers and movers of the company were the Pattons of Indianapolis. William H. Patton, educated only to the eighth grade, owned and operated the Patton Brothers Cigar Company in Indianapolis. He decided that he preferred the furniture business to selling cigars and purchased the Old Hickory Company in 1908.

Within a short time he greatly expanded the building and floor space for the manufacturing firm. He quickly brought production up to two thousand pieces a week and greatly expanded his customer base.

The Old Hickory Chair Company sent furniture to every state in the country. The National Park System bought thousands of their pieces, and today many of those pieces are still in use at such grand places as the Old Faithful Inn in Yellowstone National Park, the Grand Canyon Lodge and Grove Park Inn, a privately owned facility located in Asheville, North Carolina.

Both the New York Central and the Pennsylvania railroads had tracks leading to the doors of Old Hickory and boxcars of hickory furniture were shipped out daily. Mr. A. Richard Cohen, the owner of the local hardware store in Old Forge, New York, distinctly recalls that boxcars of hickory furniture arrived weekly and were shipped from his store to many of the camps in the Adirondacks. Cohen commented that "I had hickory company catalogues in my store and customers ordered whatever they wanted."

654PC

650PC

Old Hickory, 1941

No. 654PC Brown County Bow Back Chair
Seat 20 inches wide, 18 inches deep;
back 24 inches high; Antique Pine
arm 6 inches wide.
No. 655PC Brown County Bow Back Rocker
Seat 20 inches wide, 18 inches deep;
back 24 inches high; Antique Pine
arm 6 inches wide.
No. 650PC "Bearwallow" Chair
Seat 20 inches wide, 19 inches deep;
back 20 inches high.
No. 651PC "Bearwallow" Rocker
Seat 20 inches wide, 19 inches deep;
back 20 inches high.

655PC

651PC

At a meeting on February 8, 1921, the board of directors of Old Hickory, which included William H. Patton, his two sons George and Charles, G. A. Schnull, and Kurt Vonnegut, voted to change the name of the company to the Old Hickory Furniture Company. The *Martinsville Republican* reports that "this step was taken in order to increase the company's constantly growing business and to enter a wider field in the furniture manufacturing world."

In 1925, the Old Hickory Furniture Company catalogue featured 148 pieces of furniture that can be classified as traditional rustic hickory furnishings. They also introduced a line of painted furniture that could be ordered in either green, brown or blue. Dining chairs were listed at $4.25, and the most expensive piece was a full-size gazebo summerhouse for $300.

Marketing of the firm was accomplished through catalogues, retail department stores and traveling salesmen. The most prolific sales were at the outlets Old Hickory had in the Merchandise Mart in Chicago and the Rockefeller Center in New York City.

It is interesting to note, however, that the basic marketing nomenclature for the company changed little throughout its long history. Advertisements for the company from the early 1900s, and well into the 1950s, stresses the natural qualities of the furniture. "It is honest craftsmanship, careful and artistic . . . nature at her best . . . handmade with comfort, durability, ruggedness, and rustic charm."

Many businesses at that time were family affairs, and several members of the Patton family were involved in the management of Old Hickory. William H. Patton served as president of the firm and his three sons worked on and off for the company for many years. The Pattons have been described as an assertive family who frequently disagreed on many issues. Arguments between the four men were so frequent and disruptive that the senior Patton had to construct a soundproof office to protect the other employees from the "aggressive disagreements."

To try to alleviate matters, the senior Patton hired, around 1929, T. C. Cravens as the manager of the plant. It soon became apparent that the three sons and Cravens could not cooperate, and two of the sons eventually left the plant to pursue other careers. The two sons did, on occasion, return to the plant for short-term employment but did not stay long. In 1944, T. C. Cravens was listed as the secretary of the plant.

In September 1939, William H. Patton died. He was remembered as a well-respected businessman in the community and was noted for his membership in many organizations. He also was recognized as a very generous man whose many kind acts were not known publicly.

His son Charles became the president of the Old Hickory Furniture Company.

T. C. Cravens, a former county agent, had little experience in manufacturing but suggested new directions for the company. One of his ventures was the purchase of a farm just south of Martinsville. The farm was not considered a success, as it lost money for eighteen years in a row.

One day I happened to be driving south of town and noticed a large barn that had a sign reading "Old Hickory Farm" hanging above the door. I stopped and, with the permission of the owners, toured the barn, which is a beautiful structure. Inside were many weathered parts and relics of hickory chairs that were part of an age gone by.

In 1938, Lucy Patton, the daughter of William and an art student in Chicago, became involved in the business.

Old Hickory

No. 612-5, weight 18-1/2 lbs.

Old Hickory

No. 612-7, weight 32 lbs.

Old Hickory

No. 612-6, weight 21 lbs.

Old Hickory

No. 612-17, weight 35-1/2 lbs.

Ohio Chair Company, 1941.
No. 857PC Coffee Table. Antique Oak.
Top 24 inches in diameter, 18 inches high.

Ohio Chair Company, 1941.
No. 5169R Rocker. Antique Pine.
Saddle seat 20 inches wide,19 inches
deep. Hickory bark back 25 inches high.

Ohio Chair Company, 1941.
No. 5169 Arm Chair. Antique Pine.
Saddle seat 20 inches wide, 19 inches
deep. Hickory bark back 25 inches high.

Ohio Chair Company, 1941.
No. 650PC "Bearwallow" chair
Seat 20 inches wide, 19 inches deep.
Back 20 inches high.

She created some drawings for a rumpus room, and her family liked the idea. So, on the seventeenth floor of the Merchandise Mart, in the Old Hickory showroom, she created a wonderful den area with wagon-wheel chandeliers and rustic furniture everywhere. The exhibit was well received and described by local critics as "the grandest looking furniture" and some "of the most interesting and attractive" at the mart. Lucy Patton stayed with the company for several years and managed the Chicago outlet. For many years the showroom was located in the Merchandise Mart, but it was later moved to nearby Clark Street.

RUSSEL WRIGHT AND THE '40s INFLUENCE

As all things change, so do tastes and styles of furniture. Each decade, it seems, the Old Hickory Furniture Company introduced new styles and designs. I suspect, however, that the new styles were introduced not as complete innovations within the design department but rather as a reaction to changing tastes within society. They sought to capture a higher market share by keeping up with the ongoing trends.

Old Hickory sought influence from many of the internationally known modernistic designers, including Eric Boline, Berman Brueing and Cannis Froy. But certainly the best known of these individuals to collaborate with Old Hickory was Russel Wright.

Wright, originally from Ohio, trained in law and architecture. His credits as a designer were quite impressive, and he worked with everything from plastics to pottery to steel tube furniture and housewares. He was one of the best-known and most prolific designers of his era.

In 1941, he collaborated with the Old Hickory Furniture Company to produce an innovative series of streamlined, modern designs that were "truly an American product," as claimed by the advertisements. Wright, according to sources, named his designs Americana.

All the pieces designed by Wright had a significant 1940s look. Wright incorporated long sweeping curves into chairs, tables and settees, and often adorned his pieces with extra-long wrappings of multicolored rattan. The pieces themselves are quite different from traditional rustic hickory pieces but maintained a certain presence and are important for their incursion into modernism.

Although Wright was known to have designed many pieces for Old Hickory, it appears that his designs never achieved longevity in the offerings of the company.

Specifically, a review of the 1942 and 1956 catalogues from Old Hickory shows many pieces that are similar in design to Wright's and do have a definite modernistic flair. However, several of the exact pieces designed by Wright are not shown. At the same time, many of the pieces that are similar to Wright's designs and pictured in that era's catalogues have a large "discontinued" stamp over the piece. Consequently, one must assume that furniture with a modern look that still retained its original bark did not achieve significant favor with the public at that time.

A critical review of the pieces that were designed by Wright indicates flaws and misconceptions. For instance, Old Hickory furniture was and has been known for its ruggedness and durability. The pieces designed by Wright often appeared light and flimsy. They lacked fullness in form and seemed to be too delicate and airy. They also lacked the rugged and substantial look so pervasive in the classical rustic styles of Old Hickory.

There are other interesting stories that may shed insight into design elements within the Old Hickory company.

In an interesting interview with a former employee of Old Hickory, it was mentioned that very often several designers were invited down to Martinsville from Chicago. They were usually in residence at the plant for about two weeks and produced many different designs for consideration by the management. Upon completion of the designs, the owners of the company would review the lot and choose only a small amount that would be offered to the public.

Once the designers left, the management of the firm would then review the rejected designs and make subtle changes in the pieces, and then include them in their next catalogue. According to the former employee, the changes in the designs were made so that the Old Hickory Furniture Company would not have to pay a commission to the designer for his efforts.

Today, however, several, but not all, of the designs from that era are considered classical and desirable. Nonetheless, Old Hickory made its impression on the design world with their rugged individuality and statements about the enduring qualities of nature. This sentiment was partially obscured, and to some degree lost, with their incursion into the realm of modernism.

It should be mentioned, however, that along with the new designs, Old Hickory continued to produce their traditional rustic designs, which were eagerly accepted worldwide.

The Roosevelts had Old Hickory at the White House. Cecile B. DeMille, Frank Sinatra, Elizabeth Arden, Richard Himber and Charles Boyer acquired pieces, and even the Rockefellers had Old Hickory furniture on a penthouse terrace in Manhattan. Further, David Windsor, former King Edward VIII of England, before his abdication, furnished an entire hunting lodge in Canada with Old Hickory furniture.

In 1931, the Old Hickory Furniture Company produced a catalogue that showed some of the most innovative pieces ever offered by the firm. The catalogue is referred to as their fortieth anniversary issue. Along with their traditional designs, new forms of lamps, tables, arm chairs, settees, case pieces and upholstered items were offered that were real innovations in the field. For instance, the #5047 corner cupboard is adorned with a gallery of spindles across the top. The #30 armchair is a significant innovation in that it incorporates spindles under the arm with hoop backs. It was also the first time they offered twelve-foot trestle tables. Many of the case pieces were constructed of chestnut, not oak as had been used in the past.

But the real innovations came with their upholstered sofas and armchairs. The arms of these pieces are intricately wrapped with rattan while the pieces are also heavily adorned with spindles under the arms and front stretchers that extend to the floor. The liberal use of spindles on many of the pieces offers a fullness and depth that earlier pieces did not obtain. It was a proud year for Old Hickory.

The 1937 catalogue shows further innovations and incursions into the home furnishings market. Most obvious, however, is the use of pine as the primary wood on many of the case pieces, table tops and flat areas on the chair arms. It is also the first time they attempted to make, through distressing and abuse, new pieces look old. It was also the year that barrel furniture was introduced. This type of furniture was popular for a while but fell from grace as time went on.

Further, 1937 was the first year that the use of the Bruce Tag is evident. At that time they began using a new chemical

Ohio Chair Company, 1931 Anniversary catalogue. No. 30 Chair. Back 16 inches high above seat; seat 19 inches wide, 18 inches deep.

Ohio Chair Company, 1931 Anniversary catalogue. No. 5047 Corner Cupboard. Height 66 inches, width 2 feet 8 inches. Dark oak finish.

Ohio Chair Company, 1931 Anniversary catalogue. No. 1213 Chair. Back 19 inches high; seat 24 inches wide, 22 inches deep.

Ohio Chair Company, 1931 Anniversary catalogue. No. 1210 Divan. Back 21 inches high; seat 63 inches long, 22 inches deep. Cretonnes, crashes and weatherproof fabric samples sent upon request.

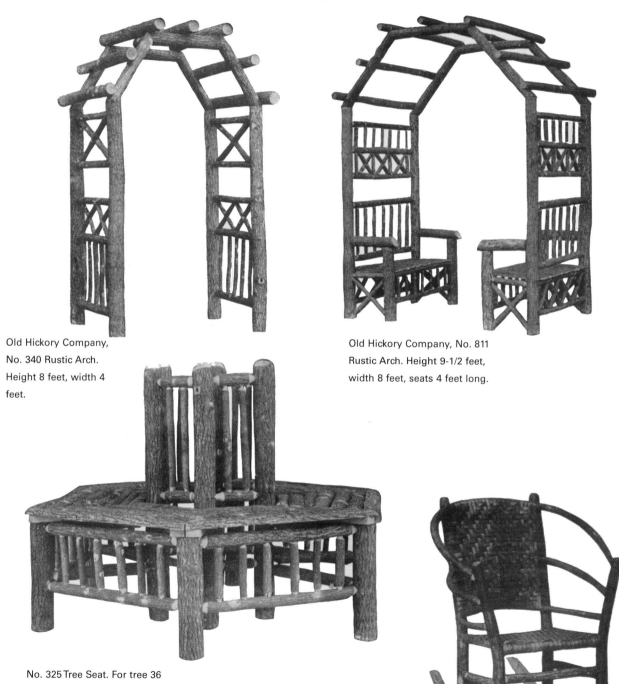

Old Hickory Company,
No. 340 Rustic Arch.
Height 8 feet, width 4
feet.

Old Hickory Company, No. 811
Rustic Arch. Height 9-1/2 feet,
width 8 feet, seats 4 feet long.

No. 325 Tree Seat. For tree 36
inches in diameter or less.

Old Hickory. Early
Andrew Jackson Rocker.

process called Bruce Preserved, which was a method of preserving the wood. On many of this era's pieces, a small, round brass tag was hammered into the chair or table leg. The tag reads "Genuine Old Hickory, Bruce Preserved." The number in the center of the circle is the year the piece was manufactured and not a model number, as is often thought.

The 1942 catalogue begins with the caveat that these products are introduced during wartime, and no guarantee could be offered as to the availability of material needed for the construction of the pieces. Nonetheless, the catalogue introduces a new line of furnishings along with advancements in their traditional rustic offerings. The American Provincial Chestnut collection includes standard interior furnishings that are indicative of the times. The collection of furnishings, in all appearances, is modern and has no bark on any of the exposed wood.

The Rustic Modern section still offered traditional rustic designs, but many new items are shown that have a classic '40s appearance. It is the first issue in which the designs of Russel Wright are shown. Many of the streamlined forms are innovative and can be referred to as modernistic. Unfortunately, the retail prices of the offerings are not available.

The 1957 catalogue further explores the American Provincial line. No bark is evident on any pieces, and the 125 pieces shown include beds, case pieces, tables, lighting, chairs and sofas.

A new line called Natural Oak is introduced in this catalogue. This line of furniture can be referred to as semi-rustic in that many of the pieces have hickory legs or posts, but some of the bark has been removed. The pulls on many of the bureaus are hickory but the main bodies of the pieces are oak. Prices for the divans go as high as $415. Desks are listed at $157, and simple spindle-back chairs are $38. Much of the furniture in

this line can be safely referred to as having a 1950s appearance.

The company that year continued to offer their traditional rustic furnishings. Many of the pieces shown still maintain a 1950s look, but the traditional Andrew Jackson chair, the signature of the company, is still offered. The price for the chair in 1957 was $36.50. Some of the pieces after 1957 did not meet with favor, as items such as tea carts, Russel Wright chairs, bars, wheelbarrow tables and folding chairs have a large discontinued stamp over their photographs.

In 1957, the company also introduced a new line called Simpatico. The pieces are very reminiscent of bamboo furniture and are often painted with a whitewash.

The barrel furniture was a successful line for Old Hickory. Few companies were making such items and "their product has found a ready made market" (*Indiana Tribune*, August 17, 1969). But the largest order ever placed with the company was for five thousand oak chairs sold to Indiana University for their library at Bloomington. The *Tribune* article goes on to say that "more than 84 persons have spent several months filling this gigantic order."

The Patton family owned the Old Hickory Furniture Company from 1908 to 1965, when it was sold to Aquamarine of Cleveland, which then merged with the Ramada Inn Corporation. At the time of the Ramada Inn ownership, the company emphasized and produced institutional furniture and was the principal manufacturer of furniture for the Ramada Inn chain. The Ramada Inn initially placed an order with the company for $300,000 worth of hotel furniture. The plans were to place another order for the same amount within the year, and then a million-dollar order in 1973. But, as things happen, the president of

Ramada Inn decided that he did not want to be in the furniture business.

Fires in August 1953 and in July 1968 destroyed parts of the factory but did not affect the productivity of the workers. James Banfield, manager of the plant, said in the July 9, 1968, *Martinsville Republican* that the "greatest difficulty experienced by the firm would be the possible loss of records locked in safes that fell through the office floor during the fire. The safes were supposed to be fireproof and this will be the acid test." No word is available to determine the efficiency of the safes.

During that same time, Old Hickory was involved in a lawsuit against the Swift Company. The suit alleged that the Swift's glue that Old Hickory had been using was faulty and failed to perform properly. The daughter of Charles Patton, Mrs. Patton-McGuinnes, remembers searching for many hours through the rubble of the fire for records relating to the lawsuit. Unfortunately, none were found.

In 1970, the company was purchased by Ralph and John Miles, a local attorney and businessman, respectively. They wanted to "restore Old Hickory's prestige" throughout the country. They sought to do this by hiring more individuals and adding sophisticated machinery. The plant at that time employed forty-two people. The Miles brothers quickly bought out a barrel factory located in Martinsville and moved the equipment to the Old Hickory factory.

In 1974, they planned to add 28,000 square feet of manufacturing space at a cost of $380,000. At this same time, 75 to 80 percent of their products were still going to Ramada Inns, and they sought to expand on the open market. During this period, the company employed sixty-six individuals and planned to add another fifty individuals to the work force. In 1976, the company had a record year,

and the new owners had hopes of doubling that figure within the year.

All things change. Trends come and go. Industries fade away. And occasionally buyers for companies cannot be found. So it was with the Old Hickory Furniture Company of Martinsville, Indiana.

The *Martinsville Reporter* on December 6, 1978, ran the following:

> The Old Hickory Furniture Company will pass into oblivion with the public auction of the machinery that made the furniture on Dec. 19. In April of this year the company was put on the market, and for lack of a buyer, on July 8, the doors were closed.

The clock and whistle at the Old Hickory plant that the townspeople set their watches to was silenced on June 3, 1975. The whistle had blown five times a day beginning at 7 a.m., at 9:45 for morning break, at noon for lunch, at 1:50 for afternoon break, and finally at 3:30 p.m. to send the workers home. This had gone on for more than sixty years.

It only seems appropriate to mention the Old Hickory Motto that was first printed at the turn of the century:

> Old fashioned comfort,
> Old fashioned days,
> Old fashioned workmanship,
> Old fashioned ways,
> Old fashioned materials,
> Old fashioned care;
> All these combined in
> An Old Hickory Chair.

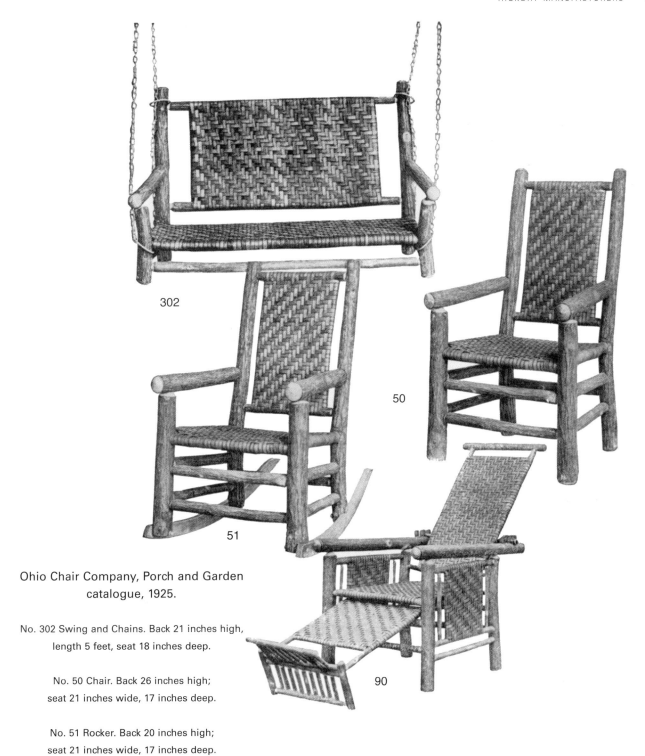

302

51

50

90

Ohio Chair Company, Porch and Garden
catalogue, 1925.

No. 302 Swing and Chains. Back 21 inches high,
length 5 feet, seat 18 inches deep.

No. 50 Chair. Back 26 inches high;
seat 21 inches wide, 17 inches deep.

No. 51 Rocker. Back 20 inches high;
seat 21 inches wide, 17 inches deep.

No. 90 Morris Chair. Seat 20 inches wide, 22 inches
deep; back 34 inches high above seat.

RUSTIC HICKORY FURNITURE COMPANY
1902 ~ 1934

The great expanse just south of the eastern shores of Lake Michigan was often referred to in pioneer days as "the mouth to the great prairies." Indeed, the French word *laporte* means "door" or "great mouth." Buffaloes once roamed there and "wild pigeons were so numerous that their flight sometimes darkened the sky." Huge tracts of native woods included white pine, ash, oak, sugar maple, elm, walnut and many other species of woods. "Beautiful sheets of water lay like mirrors and in all the west there was no more lovely region" (*History of Laporte County*, 1956).

The town of Laporte was incorporated in 1835 and became the home to many German settlers who "were of excellent stock and of sterling character." Initially, many individuals made their living in the number of sawmills that populated the area. In time, the majority of residents were engaged in some form of agriculture, either raising Indian corn, wheat, or oats or harvesting huckleberries and cranberries. With the Industrial Revolution, Laporte boasted several different furniture factories and manufacturing plants.

The Rustic Hickory Furniture Company was incorporated on January 2, 1902, and began operations in the fall. Edward H. Handley was the president and manager. Julius C. Travis was assigned to be the treasurer, and Warren Travis acted as the company's secretary.

The company was funded initially with an outlay of $35,000. The funds were raised among the three principals, but four other investors—a lawyer, a doctor, an insurance agent and a judge—also held a percentage of the business. In general, at the end of the year, after all the company's bills were paid, a dividend of 20 percent was paid to the investors. Any remaining funds would then be divided between the shareholders.

On Monday, April 20, 1903, both town newspapers reported that a fire on the previous Saturday (April 18, 1903) had destroyed the building that housed the Rustic Hickory Furniture Company. The fire was of suspicious origin and took many hours to bring under control. However, the building was totally destroyed.

It is intriguing to compare the reports of the two town newspapers. The *Daily Herald* contends that "much bungling occurred" in the attempts of the all-volunteer fire department to control the blaze. They reported that in an attempt to get the blaze under control, a hand grenade was thrown into the fire and exploded. They also mentioned several times that the building was a loss "for lack of a paid fire department."

The *Argus-Bulletin*, on the other hand, reported that the fire department "made a splendid run" to the scene. They went on to say that it was "splendid work of the companies that saved the building from being a total loss."

On October 3, 1903, the *Daily Herald* reported that "the Rustic Hickory Furniture Company is erecting a building that will double its force and capacity." The new building was located on State Street near the Pere Marquette railroad station. The new factory was to be 50 feet by 200 feet, plus

No. 52 Settee

A porch necessity. The children can romp on this without fear of breakage.

Seat 40 inches long, 16 inches deep, height of back from seat 18 inches.

No. 53—Same Settee with Rockers.

No. 20 Chair

Seat 18 inches wide, 16 inches deep, height of back from seat 22 inches.

A "lazy" chair and rocker with Rustic Hickory durability thrown in.

No. 103 Table

Stylish in its simplicity, with an auxiliary shelf for trinkets.

Height 31 inches. Oak top 30 inches square. Shelf 22 inches in diameter. Golden Oak finish.

No. 21 Rocker

Seat 18 inches wide, 16 inches deep, height of back from seat 22 inches.

an engine room, dry kiln and enough room for twenty-five employees. Goods were shipped all across North America, including to New York, California and Winnipeg. In time, forty employees worked at the company, and the 1905 *Argus-Bulletin* newspaper reported that the annual output of the firm was "no less than ten thousand pieces."

The Rustic Hickory Furniture Company of Laporte was quite successful as a business organization. Even though the company produced several retail catalogues throughout the years, they were primarily in the wholesale business.

A review of their advertising brochures indicates that their products were sold in no less than forty-seven major retail outlet stores and these stores were serviced by a number of sales representatives who had different territories around the country. The Rustic Hickory Furniture Company demonstrated great marketing strategy by allowing no more than one store in each city to sell their products. That way, stores would not compete with each other via lower pricing. Some of the top-end stores that carried their products were Mandel Bros., Chicago; Jordan-Marsh, Boston; Wanamaker's, New York City and Philadelphia; and numerous others. Every major city had outlets, including places as far away as Halifax, Vancouver, Toronto, Honolulu, and all major American cities.

I had the opportunity to correspond with Mr. Kenneth Handley, the grandson of the founder of the company, in 1989 and was also fortunate to meet and interview him at some length in April 1993.

He was a full-time employee of the Rustic Hickory Furniture Company and he writes that

this factory supplied me with a few great opportunities in my lifetime which I shall never forget. When I got

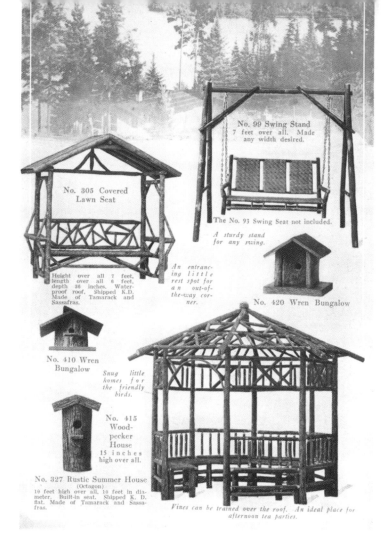

out of Indiana University in 1932—at the very bottom of the depression—I answered a letter from Glacier National Park, Montana, asking if there was someone who was willing to come out there—all expenses paid—and reweave the many seats and backs of chairs that they had in their hotel. Needless to say that I answered their letter post haste that I would be glad to come out there and give them an expert job. There was still one catch to all this . . . I had no idea how to weave a chair. It took me about two weeks to learn and then I was on my way. I spent the whole summer in the park out there and lived at Lake McDonald Hotel which was couched in the most beautiful mountain scenery you could imagine. They brought truckloads of rustic furniture to me from all the hotels in the park, so I had

Good to look at, and good to sit in. A real "cumfy" piece of everlasting furniture.

No. 80 Settee
Seat 40 inches long, 16 inches deep, height of back from seat 21 inches.

No. 36 Windsor Chair
Seat 18 inches wide, 16 inches deep, height of back from seat 22 inches.

Hickory Windsors that reflect the craftsman's skill.

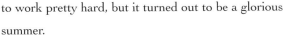

No. 101 Table
Height 28 inches. Oak top 30 inches in diameter, shelf 18 inches in diameter. Golden oak finish.

Table for the reading lamp, with a shelf underneath for the photograph album.

No. 37 Windsor Rocker
Seat 18 inches wide, 16 inches deep, height of back from seat 22 inches.

Rustic Hickory products of unusual comfort, beauty and sturdiness.

No. 68 Settee
Seat 40 inches long, 16 inches deep, height of back from seat 21 inches.
No. 69—Same Settee with Rockers.

No. 42 Chair
Seat 17 inches wide, 15 inches deep, height of back from seat 22½ inches.

No. 43 Rocker
Seat 17 inches wide, 15 inches deep, height of back from seat 22½ inches.

No. 680 Tete-a-tete
Seat 36 inches long, 16 inches deep, height of back from seat 21 inches.

A chummy bit of Rustic furniture.

to work pretty hard, but it turned out to be a glorious summer.

In the summer of 1994, I had the opportunity to visit Glacier National Park, and my wife and I stayed at the Lake McDonald Hotel. The building is a spectacular massive log structure on the shores of pristine Lake McDonald. The building and adjacent structures are full of furniture from the Rustic Hickory Furniture Company of Laporte, Indiana, and it is interesting to note that many of the chairs were rewoven from their original material and probably were done by the hands of Ken Handley some sixty years earlier.

Ken Handley was the grandson of Ed Handley, the founder of the Rustic Hickory Furniture Company. Ken Handley had two brothers, one of whom eventually became governor of Indiana. He remembers his father as never having drunk a drop of alcohol. As youngsters all three boys spent their summers working in the hickory factory. Ken's first real job with the company was that of a caner, for which he was paid forty cents per hour. "Nobody taught me how to do it . . . I just watched one of the other caners and went to work."

Handley found that the company gave him significant career direction. He writes, "When I returned to the factory, our bookkeeper had become seriously ill and was forced to quit. Because I like working with figures, I became the new bookkeeper with the help of our C.P.A. and a few books that I purchased. Actually I liked the work so well that I returned to school and received a degree in accounting. Later on, I started my own practice and opened my own office. I was able to make a very good living from this endeavor."

He remembered the Laporte factory as a "good sized but very narrow building that was powered by steam engines and very noisy." He described the plant itself as having many overhead belts that drove the machinery and many chairs hanging on hooks from the ceiling for the caners to weave. The chair caners themselves were all women because they were "more reliable than men and caning seemed appropriate for them to do." The factory was open five days a week and operated from 8 a.m. and closed in the evening at 5. Employees were paid at the end of each week.

The factory purchased second-growth hickory poles that were shipped via railroad to Laporte from southern Indiana. The trees were between three and four years old and once they reached the factory they were cut, dried and sanded prior to manufacturing. The splint used for the seats and backs of the chairs was, according to Handley, ordered from Germany.

One unique feature about the factory was that they "were a one-run outfit." The entire factory would make only one product at a time. Once that run of, say, two hundred side chairs was complete, the company would tool up for another run of a different product. There were no special orders and individuals had to wait for a scheduled run of a product. The company's efforts were to keep the warehouse fully stocked, and their busiest season was always summer. The company had only one vehicle, which was used to deliver finished products to the railroad.

There was only one in-house designer. Workers were encouraged to initiate their own designs and contribute to

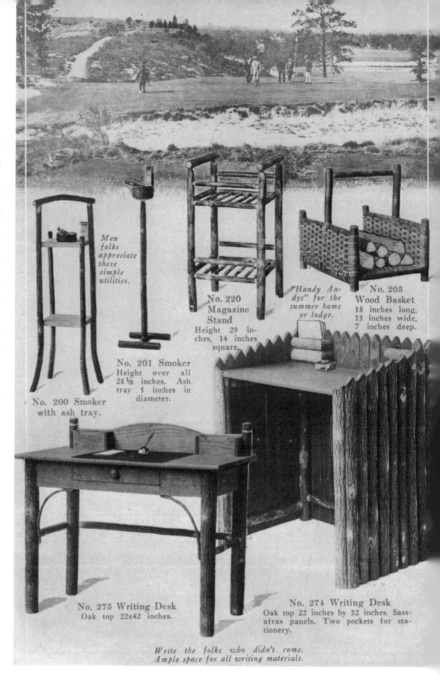

Men folks appreciate these simple utilities.

No. 220 Magazine Stand
Height 29 inches, 14 inches square.

"Handy Andys" for the summer home or lodge.

No. 205 Wood Basket
18 inches long, 13 inches wide, 7 inches deep.

No. 201 Smoker
Height over all 28½ inches. Ash tray 5 inches in diameter.

No. 200 Smoker with ash tray.

No. 275 Writing Desk
Oak top 22x42 inches.

No. 274 Writing Desk
Oak top 22 inches by 32 inches. Sassafras panels. Two pockets for stationery.

Write the folks who didn't come. Ample space for all writing materials.

product development. Their products were only used as porch and cottage furniture and no attempt was made to build furniture, such as upholstered pieces, for home interiors.

Talking with Ken Handley was one of those moments that proved to be quite magical. I had spent many years searching for materials in the libraries and newspapers, and had read his family name quite often. It was very impressive

No. 93 Swing, with Chains—Seat 4½ feet long, 18 inches deep.

No. 96 Swing, with Chains.   Seat 6 feet long, 20 inches deep.

No. 97 Swing, with Chains—Seat 6 feet long, 20 inches deep, height of back from seat 21 inches, length over all 7 feet.

What is a porch without a swing? Here are some real ones.

not fail. Their products were just not in demand.

Due to adverse economic conditions, the company was forced to close in 1934.

The designs of much of the furniture from Rustic Hickory are discernible from the other companies that made hickory furniture. Many of the armchairs and rockers produced by the Rustic Hickory Furniture Company have a characteristic splay on the front posts that support the arms. The tenons that form the joints on almost all of the pieces are significantly more tapered than other firms' joinery. Another telltale fact is that on many of their beds, hat racks and accessories pieces such as clocks, lamps and sconces there is a characteristic groove cut into the ends of the hickory poles that were part of the structure of the piece.

to correspond with him and speak directly with him. At our first meeting, we were alone in his lakeside house in Laporte, and as I asked him questions, he would pause for a few seconds as if reaching back over sixty years to seek answers to things he had not thought of for decades. With each question he seemed to smile a bit and a certain brightness came over his face as he presented his answers. He apologized several times for not offering more complete answers, as the years had clouded his memories of events so early in his life.

However, he was an eternal optimist. He mentioned at the close of our interview that even though the company closed its doors at the height of the Depression, it did

Many of the pieces also have a Mission or Arts and Crafts appearance. This was not surprising, as Laporte was very near the design center in Chicago as well as the Mission companies in Grand Rapids, Michigan. Gustav Stickley, the eminent Mission designer, was known to often use rustic pieces in his decorating projects. Many pieces of Laporte furniture are shown in his book *Craftsman Homes*, 1909. Pieces that have a Mission or Prairie School influence were heavily adorned with spindles such as the bedroom set shown in the 1910 catalogue.

Many of the Laporte pieces also had a French and, occasionally, an Oriental influence as well. A few pieces are shown that have wide sweeping curves indicative of French design, while the many pergolas, gazebos and fences show an Oriental influence.

The 1910 catalogue also shows a few pieces that were made of cedar, but, in general, pig-nut hickory was the material of choice for the Laporte company.

It is also interesting to compare prices during the thirty-year history of the company. Apparently, prices for hickory furniture increased quite a bit as the years passed by , as the #49 Steamer Chair in the 1916 catalogue is priced at $12 while the 1934 catalogue priced the same chair at $20. The 1916 catalogue shows the #108 Oval Dining Table at $20 and in 1934 it was priced at $30.

Apart from the design characteristics, the Laporte company always signed their pieces with either a brand or a pink-and-green paper label that read "Rustic Hickory Furniture Co., Laporte, Indiana."

Like many other industries, the hickory furniture business is rich in history and personalities. Many firms started from meager beginnings and with little practical experience. These same firms often changed hands, and the initiating principals moved on to other ventures.

Luther A. Simons, or simply L. A. to his friends, was not a man to be denied. He was a true entrepreneur whose persistence and tenacity led him through many different avenues within the industry.

Simons was born on February 28, 1883, in Morgantown, Indiana. As a young man he worked as a lumberman in that area. As mentioned earlier, Morgantown was probably the earliest site in Indiana for hickory furniture builders.

The September 22, 1927, *Clinton County Review* printed a story discussing a new hickory furniture company involving Simons that was to open in Colfax, and reports that "the plant is to be moved here from Morgantown." Nothing more is known of his business efforts in Morgantown or the immediate area.

J. & S. HICKORY MANUFACTURING COMPANY

Simons was talked into starting the new company by J. C. Jordan, a longtime resident of Colfax. The firm was to be called the J. & S. Hickory Manufacturing Company.

Jordan was well known in Colfax as a businessman. The May 31, 1928, *Review* describes "J. C. Jordan, local capitalist, who for years was engaged in the grain business. He is a very progressive and successful businessman." Jordan was known to have been in the Colfax area for several years, as it was also reported that he constructed and sold the Colfax Grain Elevator to another local firm in 1921.

The new hickory plant was to be located in an old shredder factory and to "employ twenty to forty men, boys and women and will operate twelve months a year" reports the *Clinton County Review*. It was estimated that the company would be able to produce "four hundred carloads of chairs a year."

Jordan was to be the president and Simons vice president. The company geared itself for success as "all new machinery was to be installed." A. A. Gill, a local contractor, constructed an addition to the plant for the new broiler and dry kiln. The building was to be steam heated "and very comfortable for the workers." Further, along with his expertise, he brought two experienced caners, a foreman and their families from the Morgantown area.

Within a month, however, Jordan had forced Simons out of the company. The December 22, 1927, *Review* identified Jordan as the president of the company and goes on to say that "Ed. L. Brown, the vice-president and sales manager, is an experienced man, coming here from Martinsville, where he organized the Old Hickory Company."

Jordan was quite an aggressive man and had demonstrated significant foresight as he also managed to acquire Elden Burnhart, formerly of the Old Hickory company, as the new chief designer for the J. & S. Hickory Company. The *Review* describes him "to be one of the best men in his line to be found anywhere. His connections with the local enterprise are highly important and the company is fortunate to have acquired his services."

INDIANA HICKORY FURNITURE COMPANY

Within a few months, Jordan was in full command of the company. By May 1928, he had changed the name of the firm to the Indiana Hickory Furniture Company.

The company was quite successful for a time. The May 31, 1928, *Clinton County Review* comments that "the Colfax plant has already established itself on the markets of the country as a superior grade to all competitors."

The *Review* goes on to inform its readers that "Mr. Jordan, owner and manager of the factory, tells us that he is months behind with orders and it is imperative that he increase the size of his plant and production." At that time there were about forty-five employees at the plant and this "force had been working overtime for weeks."

Apparently he could not fit more people into the plant, so A. A. Gill was once again contracted for a new addition that was to be 120 feet long and 40 feet wide.

The July 5, 1928, *Review* reports that "work on the new addition to the Indiana Hickory Furniture Co.'s building at Colfax is progressing very rapidly and with favorable weather, ought to be under roof by this weekend." The plant operated under reduced force and was expected to be closed for the month of August while the building was completed and the new machinery installed.

In October 1928, two fires occurred at the factory but caused little damage.

The Colfax company signed their pieces with a brand on the back leg of chairs and settees. The signature reads "Indiana Hickory Furniture Co., Colfax, Ind." At first glance, identifying Colfax pieces is often difficult. However, color seems to be an indicator. Apparently, many of the Colfax furniture pieces age a bit differently from other firms' pieces. Colfax pieces age to a very mellow, rich, golden, almost orange/brown color when left inside. This is a function of the type of varnish used on the pieces. This color and the brand are the only ways to distinguish Colfax pieces from others. I have had only fifty or so pieces of Colfax hickory. Although one might get the impression that there are many pieces around, there are far more pieces of Old Hickory and other firms' products still in existence.

On April 24, 1942, Jordan was forced to sell his company due to adverse economic conditions. The firm was purchased by the Colfax Furniture Company, a desk manufacturer. The company discontinued producing hickory furniture and concentrated on office furniture.

Little is known of Jordan's later life and there are currently no known catalogues or brochures of his product line.

COLUMBUS HICKORY CHAIR COMPANY

Luther A. Simons was a man of great persistence. Once forced out of the J. & S. Hickory Company, he regrouped and in 1929, opened a very small hickory furniture firm in Mt. Vernon, Indiana. That year was not a good year for any business, and his underfinanced company very quickly folded.

Within a year, however, he succeeded in opening the Columbus Hickory Chair Company in Columbus, Indiana. The company did quite well at that location for the next twelve years.

As conflicts arose in both Europe and the Orient, it became apparent that certain materials would become scarce or no longer available to hickory furniture makers in the United States. It was reported that Germany produced 75 percent and China produced 25 percent of the weaving material used in manufacturing in this country. As the war approached it was estimated that the total available product of rattan in this country would be depleted within two months at the then present rate of industrial consumption.

Other firms, including Old Hickory at Martinsville, began substituting nylon and canvas weaving as well as using

wood slats for the bottoms and backs of chairs and other furniture products. It was also the time of nylon stockings, and many women around the country complained that the rattan chair seats would "run and damage" their stockings.

Conscious of all this, Simons developed a thick paper mat with the consistency of flexible cardboard that became an instant success in the industry. The material, called Simonite, was made from the by-products of spruce and pine trees. Simonite came in long rolls that measured forty-eight inches wide. It was cut into three-and-a-half-inch-wide strips that were left either a natural tan color or died green or red.

The product was significantly cheaper and easier to use than rattan. Under usual circumstances "workers demanded twenty-two cents per unit for the weaving of furniture with cane (rattan), whereas the same type of workmen agreed to seven cents per unit when Simonite was used," reports the January 6, 1941, *Bedford Mail.* And it was easy to manufacture, reports the same article. They found that they could produce about three hundred feet a minute. The product was so successful that within a year of its being on the market "a total of thirty-four furniture factories are now using Simonite as an upholstery," reported the *Bedford Mail*.

The January 6, 1941, *Bedford Mail* announced that as of February 15, 1941, the Columbus Hickory Chair Company would be moving to Bedford, Indiana. Simons quite confidently boasted that "the factory will be the largest in the world engaged in the manufacture of interior hickory furniture."

The reason for the move to Bedford was reported differently elsewhere. One source reported that labor problems necessitated the move. The January 6, 1941, *Bedford Times* wrote that "due to a steady growth in business, Mr. Simons has been casting about for more spacious quarters." Both reasons for the move are probably correct, but Charles Mitchell, former bookkeeper and manager of the Simons plant, said that the move was required because the Columbus building, which Simons had been leasing, had been sold to the Cummins Engine Company.

It appears that at the time of the move, Simons also changed the name of the company to the Columbus Hickory Furniture Company to reflect the fact that more than just hickory chairs were now being produced. This was documented from the 1941–43 Bedford telephone book which listed the Columbus Hickory Furniture Company, North Third.

The new plant in Bedford was to take over an abandoned railroad warehouse and occupy "thirty thousand square feet of floor space," wrote the *Bedford Times*. The city of Bedford raised $7,000 to help with the move and offered Simons the use of the buildings at no cost in exchange for his move to Bedford.

Simons was a rather extraordinary fellow. Charles Mitchell, who still resides near Bedford, describes him as a man with "big ideas, who was not afraid to act. He was always looking for something different and sometimes things went well and other times they did not, but he was not afraid to try," Mitchell said. "Even though the office was mostly family members, I was treated like one," he commented. Employees always received gifts at Christmastime.

Simons was a responsible individual who often hired the disadvantaged, including amputees and deaf individuals, as well as many men who were older than seventy-five. Simons paid them the same wages as able-bodied workers.

His daughter, Xenia Miller, who still resides in the area, describes him as a hunter and an avid outdoors person. He traveled a great deal, mostly in the south. He enjoyed inventing things and was quite ingenious.

As the plant's only designer, he often experimented with different forms of hickory furniture. His was the only company to put linoleum tops on hickory tables and desks. Although today's tastes frown on such extremes, apparently it was easy to clean and virtually indestructible. He also experimented with different finishes and innovative designs as well. He tried various woods as the bodies of the case pieces for his furniture.

He never produced more than twenty-five different hickory pieces, however. He focused on chairs, rockers, tables, night stands, hat racks, chests and beds. His famous #69 Fireman's Special chair was his most recognized piece, and he sold hundreds throughout the area for firehouses, parks and community buildings.

He generally employed about fifty employees. Winter, however, was the slow time and occasionally it was necessary to lay off a few of the workers. His wife also worked with the firm, and she was responsible for training the women who were hired as weavers.

His company never produced catalogues, selling instead through brochures and traveling salesmen. He never signed his pieces, which is surprising because he was occasionally described as a man who liked to be listened to. "If you're right, then you're right," he often said.

Simons consistently sought new direction for his talents and products. He designed many local motels and also decorated them completely with his furniture. It was reported that he designed and decorated many of the Wig Wam motels throughout the south as well as the Horse Shoe Camp, Renfro Camp and Dutch Mill Cottages, all in Kentucky.

In 1984, I was traveling in Kentucky, and it was late at night. My usual motel was full so I drove down the road a few miles and found an out-of-the-way place that looked comfortable and, fortunately, had a flashing vacancy sign just near the driveway.

As I walked into the office area, I immediately realized that I was in one of Simons' Wig Wam motels. Hickory furniture was everywhere and I was surprised at how well the pieces had aged. There was a wonderful fifteen-foot bar, a very tall fire screen, several chairs and a desk for the manager. In the morning I asked the ninety-three-year-old owner for a tour of the motel. Each of the twenty rooms was decorated with hickory furniture from the Simons plant. The full and twin beds were still tight and each room had a dressing table, hat rack, lamp table, bureau and two armchairs.

I was fortunate to spend a few hours with the loquacious owner of the motel and, after considerable negotiation, was able to buy from him a wonderful six-foot drop-leaf dining table that was stored in a shed. A few years later, the owner called and offered me the contents of the entire motel, which I immediately purchased.

Although Simons' pieces were never signed, they are easy to distinguish from the works of other manufacturers. The chairs and rockers tend to be a bit boxy. The wood is often heavy and oversized. Most of the bark has been peeled or sanded and the pieces have a modernistic '50s look to them. The pieces, however, are rugged and strongly built.

Like all human endeavors, there are numerous stories and dramas that were played out within the Columbus Hickory Furniture Company. One of the most compelling is the tale of the bookkeeper who apparently succeeded (initially, at any rate) in embezzling $5,000 from the factory and was later caught in an audit ordered by Simons. The bookkeeper spent time in jail and was never heard from again.

Simons died in 1951. His brother Raymond ran the company for a few years but lacked the necessary business acumen to manage the firm successfully. In time, different segments of the firm were sold off. Lawrence Quick purchased the Simonite segment and moved the plant to Edinburgh, Indiana. The product, referred to today as paper weave, is still on the market.

The Columbus Hickory Furniture Company eventually closed as a result of poor management and changing tastes within society.

JASPER HICKORY FURNITURE COMPANY
1928 ~ 1938

The town of Jasper, Indiana, lies a few hours south of Indianapolis in the rolling hills of south-central Indiana. It boasts the largest Catholic church in the region, and many of its residents cut down the indigenous hardwood trees because they did not like the birds residing there.

It is a town of strong-willed individuals of German descent and a local restaurant, the Schnitzelbank, that serves outstanding knockwurst, sauerkraut and liverwurst. It is, to this day, a very clean town.

Like much of Indiana, it was an area rich in agriculture but also became a major manufacturing center. Many of the firms operating there in the early part of the century were in the furniture business, including the Jasper Cabinet Co., the Jasper Wood Products Co., the Jasper Turning Co., the Jasper Veneer Mills and several others.

John Schnaus was born on March 25, 1882, in nearby Celestine, Indiana, and before he was thirty he was the father of six. He finished seventh grade and began a career as a lumberman that quickly turned into a serious business. He helped his own father start the Jasper Cabinet Company in 1928. He was very successful, and by the time he was forty, he was either president or on the board of at least three major corporations in his community.

It is not certain what the days of John Schnaus were like, but apparently he had a full-time job in addition to his own business interests. In 1932, Robert Schnaus, the third son of John, wrote a paper for his English class at Indiana University. In the paper he describes his father: "He is at present manager of a plant in a small town about fifteen miles north of Jasper that manufactures outdoor furniture." Son Robert received only a B- for his efforts on the project. The teacher responded on the paper "not bad, except for the numerous comma blunders."

In 1928, John Schnaus organized the Jasper Hickory Furniture Company. The company had over one hundred shareholders but the principal owners were immediate family members. The board of directors was comprised of John Schnaus, Louis Eckstein, Claude Gramelspacher, Ed Koffitz and brother-in-law Adolph Egloff, of Vincennes. Board meetings were held once a month.

The firm hired a manager to run the company, but he was quickly fired for lack of business experience and ability. By the time the Depression hit, Edward Schnaus, a recent engineering graduate and son of John, was hired to run the plant. Edward Schnaus was known as a "very straight laced individual" and was affectionately referred to as "the family brain."

Within a few years, however, it became apparent that the heart of Ed Schnaus was not in hickory furniture manufacturing. He left the company and joined the Benedictines. He later received a Ph.D. in physics and taught at the university level for many years. He now resides at St. Anselms Abbey in Washington, D.C.

I have been fortunate to correspond with him and at age eighty-five he recalled the following about the start of the Jasper Hickory Furniture Company:

My father had some property in the town that he wanted to put to use, and the success of the hickory furniture plant in Martinsville, up near Indianapolis, suggested that we might try it in our furniture town to the south. We had an employee from Martinsville who had worked in the plant there and a small amount of swings and chairs were produced in Jasper; but the venture was not a success.

He [his father, John] had an interest in furniture making all his life; one of my first memories is of his dealing in hickory spokes for wood wheels of cars during the days of World War I.

The structure [of the building] was mainly brick, with concrete floor. It is still standing, now owned by the Stentfenagel family. Equipment for peeling and canning tomatoes had to be removed and some woodworking machinery installed.

In 1933, John Schnaus called his son Robert, then a sophomore at Indiana University, and asked him to take over the plant in the absence of his brother Robert.

Robert Schnaus, who died on February 6, 1994, was a very business-oriented, focused, high-energy, outgoing individual. He constantly told and played jokes amongst his family and peers, and his favorite question to anyone was "how's business?" He loved the stock market.

Like many small-town people, he was a devout family man. His daughter Helen Schnaus-Cottingham remembers that he never raised his voice to his kids. He set very high standards and all his kids were straight-A students. The family loved music and all the kids played musical instruments. "He was a great inspiration to us and even when the

river was flooded he took a boat to work." The factory was located on the Patoka River, which frequently rose above its banks and caused a serious disturbance in town.

He also had a very profound sense of humor and kept a box of funny articles and jokes that he found amusing. He was a gregarious man who enjoyed a drink and an occasional visit to the rural distilleries. He hated the I.R.S. as well as the local unions.

Robert Schnaus was a very well-liked and valuable member of the community. During his life he served as director of the German National Bank, served on the Jasper Utility Board, was on the Jasper City Council, was on the Indiana Flood Control Commission, served as Director of the National Association of Manufacturers, acted as director of the Old National Bank in Evansville, was also a Fourth Degree Knight of Columbus, was president of the Memorial Hospital Board of Directors and held many other positions of responsibility.

Upon his death, Mayor Jerome Alles of Jasper described him as "one of the movers and shakers in Jasper . . . he took time out to serve his community."

Robert Schnaus ran the Jasper Hickory Furniture Company for the last seven years that it operated. Hickory poles were cut and brought in from nearby Bristow. The Witte family cut the poles and delivered them by truck to the plant.

According to Edward Schnaus, during the first three years the company was operating, it never had more than twenty employees and occasionally went as low as three. Once the plant became busier, as many as fifty individuals were employed.

According to Mary Alice Schnaus, who worked at the

plant starting in 1932, there were only two women, Catherine Lampert and Anna Pfeffer, who did the weaving for the entire company. It took a whole day for one person to weave a glider.

At peak production, the company manufactured about two hundred pieces per week. Autumn was a time primarily for the production of juvenile furniture, and the Christmas season saw orders coming in for such items. Employees were paid twenty cents per hour, and the manager of the plant, Robert, received $50 per week.

The Jasper Hickory Furniture Company never signed its pieces, presumably because it was primarily wholesale. Stores such as Paine Furniture in Boston purchased their items and then placed their own names on the pieces.

The only known catalogue from the company shows about 160 different pieces that the company offered for sale. Each of the pieces offered was an exact copy of items produced by the more successful and prolific Old Hickory

Furniture Company of Martinsville. Such plagiarism of designs was apparently then acceptable, as no mention of lawsuits has surfaced in my research of the different firms. Occasionally, unsigned pieces of hickory have surfaced in that area, and one can only assume that they were from the Jasper plant. Despite their being copies of other companies' designs, they were very well made.

In time, however, the realities of the business climate of the 1930s caught up with the company, and the family decided to close the firm in 1938. The machinery and other woodworking tools were sold to Emerson Laughner for his new company, Indiana Willow Products, of Martinsville, Indiana.

The Jasper Hickory Furniture Company was renamed the Jasper Novelty Furniture Company and went on to successfully manufacture such items as end and coffee tables, bookcases, commodes, record cabinets and other associated accessory furniture.

HOOSIER HICKORY FURNITURE COMPANY
1927 ~ 1940

Most good businessmen are risk takers and take note of the success of others. So it was for Joseph J. Beck of Terra Haute, Indiana. Beck saw the success of the companies in Martinsville and Laporte and decided to try his hand in the hickory furniture business.

The Hoosier Hickory Manufacturing Company incorporated on December 21, 1926. Five individual stockholders were partners in the business, including Louis

Silverman, Lovell Waterman, Orlando Owen, Edmond L. Brown and Joseph Beck. This group also served as the board of directors. There were other shareholders as well, but their names are not known.

The company opened its doors in January 1927 in Terre Haute, located in the central-western part of the state. The firm's exact address was 1600 Hulman.

Beck was named president and Edmond L. Brown, who

was an early owner of the Old Hickory plant and had been recently running a Morris chair company, was named secretary. Louis Silverman was named the treasurer. The company was listed as a manufacturer of rustic furniture.

Very little is known about the company and it apparently survived only a few years. Just one piece of their furniture, a settee found in Wisconsin, has ever been identified. Fixed to the leg of the piece was a paper decal that read "Hoosier Hickory Manufacturing Co. Terra Haute, Ind."

The company seems to have changed hands, as two years later the firm was again listed in the Terre Haute phone book at the same address and phone number. This time, however, the company had new officers, including Jas. S. Royce as president, Lovell E. Waterman, vice president, Jos B. Pfister, secretary, and Keith O. Owen, treasurer. The listing goes on to read that the company manufactured porch and garden furnishings. State records indicate that in 1928 the capital stock issues were raised from $50,000 to $62,000.

No other records of the company were listed with either of the local newspapers of that time. State records indicate that the company was dissolved on January 25, 1940.

INDIANA STATE FARM INDUSTRIES
1929 ~ Present

The State of Indiana Department of Industries also had a significant influence on the hickory furniture movement. Located forty miles southwest of Indianapolis, the State Farm in Putnamville has been manufacturing hickory since 1929.

As part of their "debt to society," inmates were required to spend eight to ten hours a day in the manufacturing department. There they constructed not only brushes, mops, brooms and related accessories but hickory furniture as well.

As many as forty inmates worked on the furniture and they produced between two to three hundred pieces per week. Officially, until 1980, the items could only be sold to state agencies such as fire houses and state parks. But I suspect, considering how many pieces I have seen, that if one wanted to get prison furniture, it was accessible.

In 1980, however, the items were made available to the public. State prison furniture was exhibited in August at the Indiana State Fair and displayed at such places as Abe Martin Lodge in Nashville, Indiana.

In the 1960s, the inmate population declined and the prison ceased the manufacture of hickory furniture. Several years later, when the population increased, the farm resumed the construction of furniture made of hickory.

In the early years, the inmates constructed excellent furniture. Many of their designs were truly innovative and are considered classic today. Their #5298 bench is very desirable as is the #5299 footstool. Their "special rocker and arm chair" is considered very innovative as well and is eagerly sought after. Their #5266 "special settee" is also an innovation in design and no other company produced such a piece. They also produced excellent Andrew Jackson rockers and armchairs as well as exceptional porch gliders. Their side chairs are very well made and all the furniture is quite comfortable.

The State Farm never signed their pieces but they are easily recognizable and distinguishable from commercial products manufactured by the other hickory firms in Indiana.

Very little is known about the State Farm hickory business for understandable reasons. I must say that I have never had anyone admit to me that they "worked" at the farm. They did, however, manufacture exceptionally high-quality pieces until the mid-sixties. Today they continue to manufacture products of the same designs offered in the early years, but their pieces, unfortunately, lack the careful attention to detail and refinement that was present in the middle part of the century.

SHIRCLIFF INDUSTRIES, INC.
1935 ~ 1937

In March 1934, Shircliff Industries, Inc., a continuation of the Max Shire Company, Inc., opened its doors in Vincennes, Indiana. T. Max Shircliff was the president, J. G. Fletcher acted as vice president and Charles R. Shircliff served as secretary-treasurer. The headquarters were located in Office 402 at the American Bank in Vincennes.

The factory was located a few blocks away, in a very large building at 307 Taylor Avenue that had previously housed another furniture firm, the Vincennes Furniture Manufacturing Company. The earlier factory manufactured kitchen cabinets but fell into a state of disrepair as the business failed.

In an effort to bring more industry to Vincennes, the Chamber of Commerce and at least sixty established local businesses, including J. C. Penney, Kresges, Gardner and Sons, Thompson Grocery, Smittie Super Service, and others, con-

tributed to the rehabilitation of the building for the new firm.

On June 4, 1935, the *Vincennes Post* reported that "all necessary supplies were purchased in Vincennes for the rehabilitation of the building and Vincennes labor employed . . . to carry out the diversified business of . . . Hoosier Hickory and rustic furniture."

Diversified investment significantly improved the quality of the factory. "New facilities in the area of window lights, lighting, equipment, plumbing and other conveniences" had been added, reported the *Vincennes Post*. The first floor had a mill room with "adequately equipped machines" that handled the various steps in preparation and assembling of hickory furniture. The *Post* also stated that "the second floor with large and airy rooms and white washed walls includes the department devoted to the weaving of rattan seats in the hickory furniture."

Supplies for the company were ordered from other Vincennes firms and the plan was to "secure the hickory and sassafras tree poles for supply of the plant from this section of the state which is said to be plentiful in this area. The rattan used for the chair seats is imported from Japan, the bark used for that purpose and the interior . . . [of the rattan plant] . . . used for basket weaving," wrote the *Vincennes Post*.

The business met with initial success as they sold their products in the South, East and Midwest. The company had their own salesmen located in cities such as Kansas City, Nashville, Columbus, Cincinnati and New York City.

The company not only made Hoosier Hickory Furniture but also manufactured baskets that were sold nationally.

The only known photo of the company was sent to me by Mikey Wood, the great grandson of the manager of the plant, Joseph Bahr. An uncle of Wood, also an employee of the Shircliff company, mentioned that the pay for a laborer in 1937 was $9 a week. Employees worked nine hours on weekdays and five hours on Saturday. The *Vincennes Sun* on May 20, 1934,

reported that "the company had been brought to life again and is providing employment for 35 or more local workmen."

It is very difficult to identify furniture made by Shircliff Industries. I have never seen a piece of Shircliff furniture with any sort of signature and it is doubtful that the company signed any of its pieces. However, from the pictures shown, I have had a number of diminutive side and armchairs that match the pieces presented. The chairs are slightly smaller in scale than pieces from other hickory furniture companies but are exceptionally sturdy and well built.

At first, the company showed great promise as "furniture by the carload and baskets by the thousands already have left the plant in the few short weeks it has been in existence," reported the *Vincennes Sun* in 1934. Nonetheless, the company only survived a few years making hickory furniture and baskets. The 1937 *Vincennes City Directory* lists the company as "Manufacturers of Floral Baskets and Supplies, [and] Hickory Furniture," while the 1939 directory lists the company as "Manufacturers of Carbonated Beverages and Beer Wholesalers."

INDIANA WILLOW PRODUCTS COMPANY, INC.
1937 ~ 1963

In the early 1930s, both Clyde C. Hatley and Emerson D. Laughner were employees at the Old Hickory Furniture Company in Martinsville. Hatley was employed as the foreman in the weaving department and Laughner worked in sales and bookkeeping starting in 1926. Like many men,

they were laid off from their jobs in 1932 due to the severe economic conditions brought about by the Depression. Little is known of Hatley other than he became the organizer, president and driving force behind the Indiana Willow Products Company, Inc., also of Martinsville.

Indiana Willow was incorporated on February 23, 1937. Hatley was the head man, while Laughner served as secretary. Another longtime Martinsville resident, Smith Johnson, was also a partner. Although records indicate that Johnson was an investor and full board member, he was not an employee of the company. His wife, Crissy, however, worked for the company for many years.

A fourth individual, R. R. Kinton, was also an investor in the firm but was neither a board member nor an employee.

The four men invested $1,950 in one hundred shares of common stock for the company. Each share was valued at $19.50. Both Johnson and Laughner owned twenty-five shares each. Hatley owned twenty-four and Kinton owned twenty-six.

According to their Articles of Incorporation, the new company was to "manufacture and sell furniture and like products." Weekly salary for Hatley was $20. Salary for secretary Laughner was $10 per week. Initially, in an attempt to distance themselves from Old Hickory, the company was to use willow as the frames for their products. But in a short time it became apparent that willow was scarce and difficult to acquire, so they reverted to the use of hickory as the principal wood for their furniture.

Indiana Willow immediately purchased several lots in the new Special Machinery and Foundry Company's addition, an industrial park in the city of Martinsville. The five lots cost them $1,200 plus 6 percent interest over five years. In time, two more lots were purchased, and a large building was acquired that housed the company for the twenty-six years they were in business.

Laughner was a very knowledgeable individual and was aware of the financial difficulties of the Jasper Hickory Furniture Company. Consequently, when Jasper closed in 1938, he was able to purchase all the equipment from the plant and used it for his new company in Martinsville.

Emerson Laughner was a very friendly, open man. I was very fortunate to have spent many hours with him over the years, and his insight and contribution to the documenting of the Indiana hickory business has been immense. I remember him as having an infectious smile, and he was certainly one of the most loquacious individuals I have ever met. The first time I met him he spoke for three hours, nonstop.

I also remember spending time with him at his house. One day he was showing me a few things in his garage and out of a box he produced an original branding iron from the Old Hickory Furniture Company. Both of us being curious, we decided to plug the iron into a nearby electrical outlet. We were both quite shocked (no pun intended) when sparks flew and all the lights in the house and garage went out. Needless to say that his wife, Bertha, was quite upset about it and told us so. We did not realize that the iron was wired for 220 volts and not 110 as most common wiring is set for. We spent the next half hour replacing fuses in the basement of their home.

On another occasion, while sitting in his office, he showed me several photos of his company displaying their merchandise at trade shows during the mid-1940s. I mentioned to him I was very interested in the photos and he assured me that he would leave them to me in his will.

Sadly, Emerson Laughner was killed in a car crash in 1993 at age ninety. A few months after his death, I received a large box in the mail. The box contained not only the photos, but all the financial records and legal documents from the Indiana Willow Products company. His niece mentioned

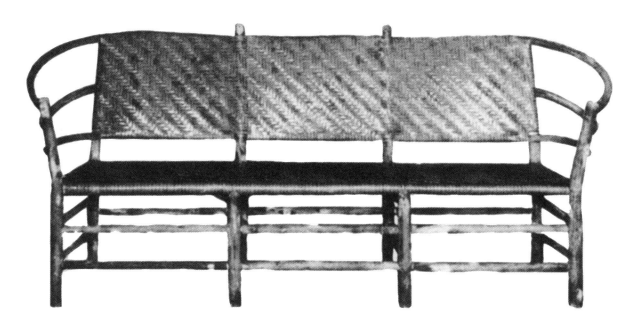

Indiana Willow, No. 67 Settee. Seat 72 inches
long, 20 inches deep, 21 inches high.

Indiana Willow, No. 47 Chair. Back 33 inches
high; seat 20 inches wide, 19 inches deep.

Indiana Willow, No. 67 Rocker. Back 20 inches
high; seat 19 inches wide, 18 inches deep.

in her letter that she thought that I might like to have the records to the company as well.

The documents included the initial papers and articles of incorporation, all the financial records for the twenty-six-year history of the company, stocks, extensive lists of customers, complaint letters and numerous other papers that carefully depict the history of the firm.

In time, Indiana Willow did extensive business throughout the country. Their very first sale was to the William H. Block Co. of Indianapolis for a total of $151.34—less a discount of $3.03. The first official deposit from a customer was for $148.31. Total deposits for the first month they were in business were $1,715.85. The records indicate that the company sold locally to retail stores in the nearby towns of Greencastle and Brazil, Indiana, as well as to companies in the nearby states of Illinois, Ohio, Wisconsin, Pennsylvania and Michigan.

The following month, business was better. Total sales for that month were $2,120.76, and their customer base had dramatically expanded. Records show forty-two major sales to such companies as Reliable Furniture, Roberts Furniture, Horace Link Co., Kings Billiard Co., Kaufmans Department Store, J. L. Hudson Co. and many others.

As the year progressed, business definitely slowed down. Receipts for August 1937 were $335.89 and went to a low of $105.26 in March 1938. Total sales for their first year in business were $6,507.81. Total sales for second year in business (1938) were $8,612.46.

Business continued to fluctuate, but their customer base was expanding. In April 1939, they listed customers such as Bloomingdale's, the Boy Scouts of America, Carson, Pirie, Scott and many others. Receipts for that month totaled

$2,057.44. It is also interesting to note that the Jasper Novelty Furniture Co., formerly the Jasper Hickory Furniture Co., which went out of business just the month before, began purchasing hickory furniture from Indiana Willow.

As the years went by, the company grew. The July 1943 customer list mentions John Wanamaker's of Philadelphia, F. A. O. Schwarz of Boston and Macy's of New York City. Sales for that month were $2,040.11.

The acquisition of the Wanamaker account by Indiana Willow was a source of great pride for Emerson Laughner, and as he told the story he had a brightness in his eyes and a smile on his face.

Laughner traveled to Philadelphia each fall on the *Spirit of St. Louis* train to meet with clients and generate new business. He had tried for four years to sell his products to Wanamaker's of Philadelphia, but they had a long-standing account with Old Hickory, also of Martinsville.

In 1942, however, Laughner was invited into the office of Mr. McDonald, the buyer at Wanamaker's. McDonald was on the phone with Charlie Patton of Old Hickory and he was very concerned because his order had not been filled in almost a year. At the end of the phone conversation, McDonald was so irate that he cancelled all his Old Hickory orders and slammed down the phone. He then turned to Laughner and asked to see a sample of his products. Laughner had a chair shipped overnight to McDonald. Once the chair arrived, Laughner presented it to McDonald, who picked up the chair and threw it down the hall. Inspecting the chair and seeing that it was not damaged, McDonald placed a very sizable order that was renewed for many years with the Indiana Willow Products Company of Martinsville, Indiana.

I recall that Emerson Laughner took great pride in this sale, probably because Charlie Patton of Old Hickory had fired him a few years earlier.

Emerson Laughner frequently relied on a unique business intuition and told the following story to me:

In 1940, Wendell Wilke was running for the presidency of the United States and he had scheduled a large parade and rally for himself in Elwood, Indiana. This was to be a very large event and the town expected 250,000 people to attend. One night, about a week before the event, I had a dream that if I could make hickory stools for the spectators, well, a lot of money could be made. When I arrived at the plant that morning we did not have the correct amounts or sizes of wood to construct the type of stool I had in mind. Well, I went out and found a good supply of sassafras poles that would suffice for the materials for the stools. I had the employees work day and night for six straight days making sassafras stools. The day of the event I borrowed a large tent from the local funeral home and set up in a vacant lot in Elwood. The day of the event we sold 700 stools in an hour and a half and made a handsome profit, and all this happened because I had a dream.

On several occasions I have found, and currently own, one of Emerson's sassafras stools that not only commemorate Wendell Wilke Day in Elwood but also Mr. Laughner's dream.

The 1948 catalogue of the firm's offerings pictures seventy-nine items. Many of the items were similar to items offered by Old Hickory, but Indiana Willow introduced many innovations that were true advancements in the design of hickory furniture. For instance, Laughner introduced a change in the original Andrew Jackson chair by extending the upper hoop completely across the top of the back legs, thus making the chair easier to construct and advancing the aesthetics of the design as well. He was also the first to introduce new patterns in the weaving of the seats and backs of the chairs and beds that his company offered. Further, the number 47, 52 and 96 chairs are complete innovations in the field. The chairs are considered classics and are very much desired by collectors today.

Laughner resisted the temptation to experiment with designs that would show an influence of the '40s and '50s. Instead he stuck with what could be called the traditional look for rustic Indiana hickory furniture. I have had the opportunity to examine many of the pieces from the Indiana Willow shop and have found them to be very well made and quite comfortable and functional.

Emerson used to perform what he called the "quarter test." On occasion he would wander back into the finishing room and bounce a quarter off the top of a table or other flat surface. If the quarter left no mark, it would pass inspection. If it did leave a mark, the piece was rejected and sent back for refinishing.

Laughner also mentioned to me that the employees involved in the construction of the furniture were "real characters." During the 1950s, he had a woman working at the plant who was responsible for weaving three-inch-wide strips of nylon onto the seats and backs of chairs. "She was incredibly fast," reports Laughner. "She was a large, fat

Indiana Willow, 1948

Clockwise from upper left:

No. 96 Rocker. Back 24 inches high; seat 19 inches wide, 18 inches deep.

No. 96 Settee. Back 24 inches high; seat 42 inches wide, 18 inches deep.

No. 52 Chair. Back 20 inches high; seat 19 inches wide, 18 inches deep.

No. 47 Chair. Back 33 inches high; seat 20 inches wide, 19 inches deep.

Indiana Willow, 1948

No. 200 Swing and Stand. Swing seat 42 inches long, 18 inches deep. Overall height 7 feet.

No. 930 Couch. Length 82 inches, width 29 inches, height 20 inches.

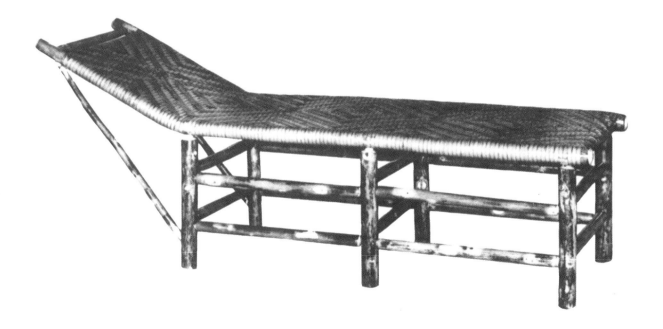

woman who always had a mouth full of chewing tobacco. Well, she would put a handful of tacks in her mouth at the same time and spit out the tacks that she needed to nail down the webbing. It was an awful sight but she was fast and got the job done."

Soon after the story was told to me, I acquired a mint-condition, three-piece set from the Indiana Willow shop that was woven with nylon webbing. It was interesting to note that around each nail holding down the webbing were dark brown stains that were obviously from the "fat lady in Martinsville with the chewing tobacco."

Emerson Laughner was a very well-liked man who could sell an Eskimo suntan lotion. He not only ran a successful business but was also secretary of the Martinsville Chamber of Commerce. In 1951, the Midwest Parlor Furniture Company, Inc., was looking around for a site for their factory. They had traveled over eight thousand miles throughout the Midwest searching for the right place for their firm. Although they were looking for a larger building, the June 1951 *Business and Industry* magazine reports that they were "convinced of the potentialities of the local site by Mr. Laughner." The company moved in and prospered for many years.

PROBLEMS

There is no business, however well conceived, that does not have its fair share of problems. On July 5, 1953, Sid Luckman wrote to Emerson complaining that a hickory fence constructed by Indiana Willow Products was "falling apart . . . it is no longer a fence but an eaten up, rickety, rotted, unsafe railing." He threatened to take action and see "higher authorities."

Laughner discussed this problem with his sales manager, Harry M. Wolfe of Chicago, who stated that "there must be some reason for that fungus to be accumulating there. That is something over which we have no control, and I think that we should tell him just that." As time went on, several other letters of complaint were received from the customer and their decorator.

Laughner writes back that "we do not believe that it would be of any value to replace the fence as the same condition would no doubt occur." More complaints followed, as well as a demand that the fence be replaced. Wolfe advised Emerson, "I wouldn't do anything about it." Laughner wrote back in September, "We believe that the year-round dampness of the lake is responsible for the condition the hickory is in and we do not believe that replacing the fence will remedy the matter."

More letters followed and lawsuits were threatened. The customer's lawyer, Frank Jacobson, demanded $1,067.95 for the fence, trucking and headache money. On November 27, 1953, Jacobson again wrote to Emerson and stated that he would "be compelled to institute suit against your company. . . ." The lawyer for Indiana Willow, Gilbert Butler, wrote back and concluded that ". . . We are compelled to deny liability." In all, over thirty letters were sent back and forth and, unfortunately, we are denied the full pleasure of the final outcome to the situation as no further letters or references discussing the solution have been found.

EDMOND (EDWIN) LLEWELLYN BROWN

Edmond Llewellyn Brown, born March 10, 1873, was associated with at least four different hickory furniture manufacturers. He was one of the original owners of the

Old Hickory Chair Company. He was the first head sales-man for Indiana Willow Products. He was the secretary for the Hoosier Hickory Furniture Company and also a board member and vice president of the Colfax Hickory Furniture Company. In between all this, he owned a company that manufactured Morris chairs.

Ed Brown was born in Little Rock, Arkansas, and was, according to family members, a hard-working man all his life. According to local Genealogical Descent records, he was the son of Judge Benjamin C. Brown of Memphis, Tennessee.

Brown moved to Ohio and was, for a while, a potato farmer. He then moved to Minnesota and finally to Martinsville, Indiana, where he involved himself in the hickory furniture business. He married Lucile Huxley on October 23, 1895, and served in the Spanish-American War. He was dearly loved by children and spent much time with his family. He and his wife had only one child, Francis Brown, who became a medical doctor and practiced into her nineties.

He was further described as a persistent man who would not take no for an answer. While selling in New York City for the Indiana Willow Products Company, he was calling on a buyer whom he noticed was sleeping at his desk. The buyer's secretary refused to let Brown into the buyer's office or to wake him. After over an hour of waiting, Brown walked aggressively into the office and woke the buyer. Brown shouted, telling him that he was the "laziest buyer I ever met. . . . Don't you know that time is money?" He then placed his business card on the desk but the now-irate buyer instantly tore it up. Brown then shouted that business cards cost money and the buyer threw a nickel to Brown saying that he wouldn't give two cents for his card. Brown, not to be outdone, then took out another card and placed it on the desk saying that his cards were two for a nickel and stormed out of the office.

The buyer was immediately impressed with the assertiveness of Brown and had his secretary chase him down the hall, where he was invited back to the buyer's office. After a few minutes of discussion, a significant order was placed with the Indiana Willow Products Company and was renewed for many years.

It should also be mentioned that Ed Brown was very hard of hearing. It must be assumed that Brown did not see this as a handicap as it did not impede his efforts or production. The first year he sold for the Indiana Willow Company his commissions were $1,101.61, which was more than twice what the president of the company earned. The second year (1938) he made $856 and the third year he jumped to $1,591.87. This last figure is three times the amount that Emerson Laughner made for the total year. Ed Brown died in June 1951 after a long illness.

On January 30, 1950, the board of the Indiana Willow Products Co., Inc., voted to change their name to the Indiana Hickory Furniture Co., Inc. This was done to accurately reflect the fact that their furniture was now being made of hickory and not willow. Although chairs, rockers, table bases and beds were still being made of hickory poles, the company started using maple, birch and poplar for tabletops instead of oak, as they and the other hickory companies had been using for years. "The oak wood just got so expensive that we had to make substitutes," explained Laughner. They also started using different sorts of pressed board for the backs of their case pieces such as bureaus and dressers.

During this time, however, business remained steady. They averaged around twelve employees during the warm,

Indiana Willow, 1948.
No. 320 Bunk Beds. Height
68 inches, width 39 inches.

Indiana Willow, 1948.
No. 500 Chest. Height 49 inches,
top 18 inches x 39 inches.

Indiana Willow, 1948. No. 442 Gate Leg Table. Top 18
inches wide, 42 inches long (closed). Top 42 inches wide,
60 inches long (open). Height 30 inches.

busy seasons and dropped to an occasional low of four or five people in the dead of winter. In 1955, Clyde Hatley and Emerson Laughner received a yearly salary of $3,120. Taxes for each individual that year were $332.80. Each individual also bought yearly savings bonds at a cost of $6.40 per week.

It was during this period that Emerson Laughner traveled to Florida "just to see what was going on." While down there he could not help but notice the large numbers of homes that had cheap aluminum chairs and lounges on their porches. He noticed how light in weight they were, as well as their cost, which was between $3 and $5 per chair. He also saw that the chairs could easily be stored in a car trunk or

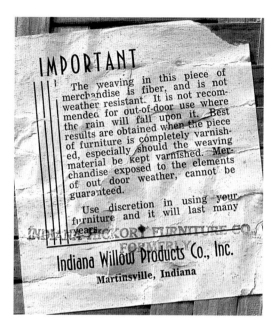

station wagon.

When he got back to Martinsville, he mentioned to Clyde Hatley that "the writing was on the wall." He knew that the hickory furniture business, his company, was in for "some rough times ahead." He also suspected that the industry would not be around in ten years.

Emerson Laughner was quite correct in his assumption: the Indiana Hickory Furniture Company, Inc., was dissolved on December 16, 1963. The properties were sold and the shares of stock were cashed in by the five remaining stockholders, including Emerson Laughner (twenty-five shares), Crissy Johnson (fifty shares), Clyde Hatley (twenty-four shares) and John Hoadley, who also held fifty shares.

THE LEGACY

Despite its demise during the 1950s and 1960s, the legacy of the Indiana hickory furniture movement lives on. The designs of many pieces that were manufactured by the various companies are now considered classic and stand as objects of art along with those from other disciplines. Many of the really great forms produced are quite rare and I know of their existence only from photographs. The very rare pieces were, at the time of their construction, very

expensive and a catalogue of many of the pieces shown in this book, to my knowledge, was never produced. The line of furniture was probably dropped because few people could afford the high cost.

The glory years of the industry, in terms of design, certainly were from its inception in the 1890s until the mid-1930s. Many great pieces were made after that period, including items made by Emerson Laughner and his company, Indiana Willow Products, but the classic forms from the early years live on and are taking their rightful place within the art world today.

This is not to suggest that the companies did not continue with their innovations. Old Hickory frequently sought innovations in its designs and repeatedly brought out new forms with which to expand their markets and explore the possibilities within their artistic discipline.

The real meaning and essence of the hickory furniture movement is its association and closeness with things natural. It brought people closer to nature and its rugged individuality set us apart from the work world and society in general. In that it was commercially made and relatively inexpensive, it allowed individuals from all across the spectrum of society to own their share.

As different forms were introduced, their creators sought to mimic current trends and to idealize the technological and stylistic advances as they evolved throughout the world. Many times these forms, even though they were developed by internationally respected designers and were unique, failed to capture the real essence and meaning of the notion of rustic. The pieces failed to capture the viewers' imaginations and did not meet the inherent qualities and meanings offered within the rustic and naturalistic realm.

There is something standoffish about rustic furniture. It is a slap in the face to high technology and society, and it exists just outside of the mainstream of civilization. When modernistic designs of hickory furniture were presented, they assumed a posture too close to technology and distanced themselves from the real meaning of rustic.

There is something almost evil, grotesque, mystical, fun and awe-inspiring inherent in nature. There are elements within nature (and us) that frighten us and yet we know that these are our roots. As we look and study the gnarls and twists inherent in organic materials, we are fascinated with its freedom and its almost total disregard for convention. We often seek and need that freedom.

We long to explore our closeness with nature and its meaning to us as individuals. It is a part of us that we so often deny and yet at every opportunity we respond to its calling. We fill our homes with plants and animals and marvel at storms and sunsets.

Hickory furniture was, in essence, simple yet elegant. It did not try to deceive us. It is what it is. It was not manipulated in the name of technology. It was made for the masses by simple men who sought self-expression in their daily efforts.

Unfortunately, even though hickory wood is exceptionally strong and durable, the majority of pieces have met their demise due to exposure to the elements, neglect and fire.

In many circumstances, the very essence of being on vacation brings about the notion of neglect toward a great many things, and rustic furniture was certainly one of them. If left out in the rain and sun, in reality, all wood sooner or later will return to the earth. It is only organic material and time takes its toll on all things.

After the Old Hickory Furniture Company at Martinsville stopped making rustic hickory chairs, they were deluged with requests to resume production. Unfortunately, they did not meet that demand and the industry sat idle for thirty years. In the mid-80s the Old Hickory Company was revived and today at least three companies, as well as the state prison in Putnamville, are once again manufacturing rustic hickory furniture. The legacy continues.

HICKORY FURNITURE GALLERY

Facing: This magnificent three-person settee, signed Old Hickory, is probably from the 1940s. It is woven with a combination of hickory strips and rattan.

Above: This table lamp, signed Old Hickory, is covered by an antique mica shade.

Facing: This small desk first appeared in the 1922 Old Hickory catalogue. It is 36 inches wide and contains a center drawer and bookshelf ends. The small wall mirror is unsigned and was probably made by the Jasper Hickory Furniture Company of Jasper, Indiana, in the early 1930s. The table lamp and side chair are also Old Hickory.

Above: This mint-condition, full wraparound Old Hickory armchair is complete with intricate herringbone weave. It appeared in the 1931 Old Hickory catalogue. The eight-sided table has wrapped legs and a cross stretcher to support the base. A set of Old Hickory toys sits on the table along with an Old Hickory table lamp.

Below: The liberal use of spindles between the leg stretchers on this table indicates a strong influence of the earlier Arts and Crafts period. First appearing in the 1914 Old Hickory catalogue, the table sold originally for $11. The hammered-copper table lamp was made by Michael Adams.

Below right: This nest of end tables appeared in the 1942 Old Hickory catalogue. Showing a flair in the legs, the tables are a precursor to the lavish fifties style. The tables have oak tops.

Opposite: This paddle-arm chair with upholstered cushions was in my collection for many years. Durable and comfortable, the chair was the site of many late-afternoon winter naps for the author.

This tall-case clock was produced by the Rustic Hickory Furniture Company of Laporte, Indiana. A variation of this clock appears in their 1928 catalogue. The actual clockworks are from the Arts and Crafts period, between 1902 and 1912.

This set of seven-spindle hickory chairs has been rewoven with western rawhide. The desk is from the early 1930s.

This early settee with open weave was constructed from
either sassafras or yellow willow. A collection of high-drama
Navajo rugs rests on the settee.

A top-condition chaise lounge from the Rustic Hickory Furniture Company sits in a loft bedroom. Numerous other antique hickory pieces complete the room.

The Old Hickory Furniture
Company made this con-
temporary entertainment
center. The pine body is
trimmed with hickory
saplings.

Above: This lounge room at an Indianapolis golf course is complete with many pieces of contemporary hickory furniture.

The golf course also houses this impressive bar and stools made by the Old Hickory Company in Shelbyville.

Many early lodges, inns and resorts around the country have significant collections of hickory furniture. The front porch of this Adirondack inn is the home of nearly a hundred pieces of hickory furniture.

Facing: This early porch glider hangs from its frame by chains and probably dates to the early 1930s. Signs and other antique rustic accessories complete the setting.

Above: This is the kitchen/island area of
Kamp Kylloe, my Lake George summer
home. The tall hickory bar stools serve as
seating for the many dinners and gatherings
at the home. A moose antler chandelier with
antique green case glass shades lights the
area.

Right: This spindle footstool appeared in the
1930s. The Old Hickory brand is evident on
the front leg.

Above: This living room set with wrapped arms was featured in the Fortieth Anniversary Old Hickory catalogue in 1931. The set is upholstered in period Permatex and Dupont fabric and features internal coil springs.

Left: This full-wrap armchair and matching footstool complement the hickory bookcase.

A woven-sided table is complete with oak top.

Facing: This hickory Windsor chair and twenty like it were found at an auction in Wisconsin. The antique shade adds a sense of intrigue to this sitting area.

When I found this rare set of eight X-brace side chairs in a basement in Martinsville, Indiana, they were in mint condition, having aged to a rich golden brown. Dating probably from the 1940s, the chairs are small and were woven with strips of hickory. The eight-foot dining table is complete with a barn-board top.

Left: The ornate antique mica shade on this classic five-pole hickory floor lamp dates from the 1920s.

Below: Eight of these hickory trestle tables were found in an old American Legion Hall in Indiana. A set of sixty-four side chairs came with the set. The unsigned table and chairs were probably made by Shircliff Industries, Inc., hickory furniture company in the mid-1930s. The chairs have an open-weave pattern on the seats and backs.

Facing: This is the original foreman's desk used in the Old Hickory factory between 1905 and 1920. I found the desk in a basement in Martinsville, home of the original Old Hickory factory. Today the desk resides in my study and is the home of hundreds of pieces of antique hickory ephemera.

This corner cupboard from the early 1930s houses a collection of small trophies. The piece was made from dimensional hickory lumber and hickory poles.

Facing: Often misattributed to Old Hickory, this bed and thousands
more like it were made by the Columbus Hickory Furniture
Company, whose owner was Luther A. Simons, the inventor of
Simonite. The beds and related furniture graced hundreds of rooms
at the Wigwam Motel chain, a popular sleeping place from the
1940s on. The beds, rockers and other seating were, of course,
woven with Simonite.

Above: This three-way mirrored dressing table was made in the
1920s by the Old Hickory company. The chair was manufactured at
the Indiana Prison in Putnamville, Indiana.

This tall-back hickory armchair appeared in the 1926 Rustic Hickory Furniture Company catalogue. It originally sold for $13.

Arguably the most rare of all the hickory bureaus, this chest is complete with woven-front drawers. Made for a cabin in the Adirondacks in 1926, the chest is part of a large collection of original Old Hickory pieces that have stood, unmoved, since their delivery in 1926!

This desk today sits in my office and serves as storage space for a mountain of papers that I'll probably never read. The piece was made by the Indiana Willow Products Company of Martinsville in the 1940s.

Facing: This tall-back hickory "comb back" rocker dates from the first years of the Old Hickory company. First appearing in 1901, the rocker was woven with hickory strips, as were all hickory seating products at that time. The dramatic antique floor lamp with a hickory-strip shade is unsigned. Other antique hickory pieces complete the setting.

Facing: Several antique hickory pieces and other rustic accessories are a natural complement to this small cabin setting.

Above: These "Bearwallow" armchairs began appearing in the early 1940s. Strong and comfortable, they were usually woven with an open-weave pattern.

Facing: This bureau from the Old Hickory company appeared in several of their old catalogues beginning in the early 1920s. The Old Hickory company never dovetailed its drawers, nor did any of the nine other hickory furniture-manufacturing firms.

Left: A classic tall, five-drawer chest from the Indiana Willow Products Company. The owners of the firm—Emerson Laughner and Clyde Hatley—were both former employees of the Old Hickory company. Having been laid off from work in 1932, they began and ran their successful company between 1937 and 1963. The drawers of this chest and most of the case goods were butt jointed and made from solid oak. Drawer bottoms were made from sheets of laminated wood product.

Below: This full-size 1920s bed is from the Rustic Hickory Furniture Company. Beds from this firm are distinguishable by the groove cut near the top of the posts as well as pencil-point post ends.

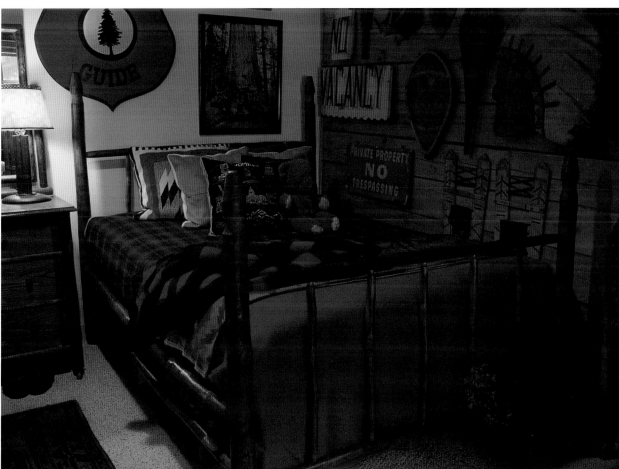

Above left: This small hickory log holder is woven with hickory strips and today serves as a magazine holder

Left: This magazine rack, woven with Simonite, was featured in the Indiana Willow Products Company catalogue in 1948. The Bedford, Columbus and Indiana Willow Products companies are the only firms known to have used Simonite. During my thirty years of collecting and researching hickory products, I have never seen an antique piece from the Old Hickory company that had Simonite as its weaving material. However, the Old Hickory company of today, presently located in Shelbyville, often uses the product. They refer to it as Vintage Weave. It is the same product invented in the 1940s by Luther A. Simons.

Above: This magazine stand was featured in the 1931 Old Hickory catalogue. I paid $60 for the piece many years ago at a second-hand store in South Bend, Indiana.

This rare, mint-condition armchair appeared in the 1931 Old Hickory catalogue. The hammered-copper table lamp is by Michael Adams.

Below: This small, six-sided tabourette hosts a hand-carved moose.

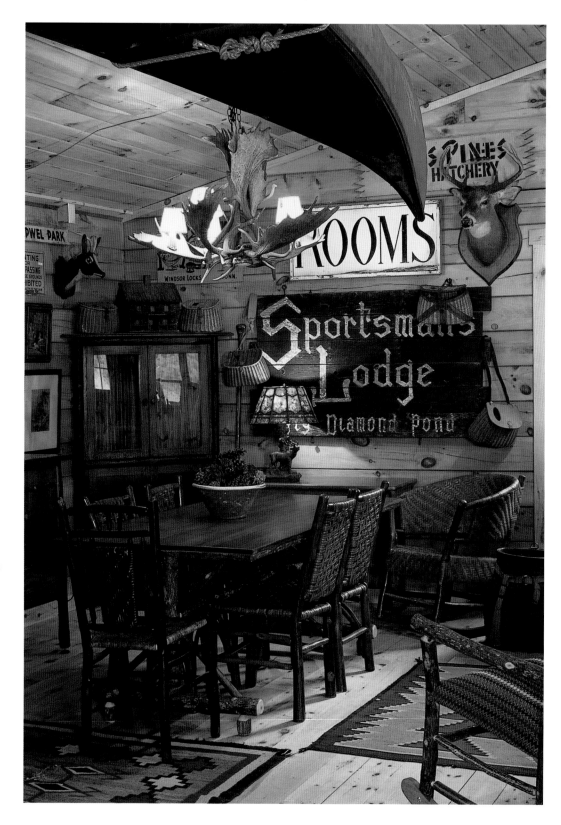

Numerous pieces of hickory furniture and antique rustic accessories blend to make a dramatic statement regarding rustic style.

The living room at the home
of the author. The large cabinet is an entertainment center.

Facing: Neatly lined up and always in use, these spindly rockers rest on the front porch of the Roosevelt Lodge in Yellowstone National Park. The 1929 Old Hickory catalogue offers the armchair for $10 and the rocker for $11. They first appeared in the 1922 catalogue.

A classic back porch in the Adirondacks is furnished with numerous pieces of antique hickory furniture, making a comfortable setting for the owners to watch dramatic sunsets and the occasional passing bear.

Contemporary furniture from the Old Hickory
company complements a variety of rustic set-
tings. The contemporary sideboard was reintro-
duced by the company a few years back and
continues to be well received by the public.

Referred to as a "Divan" by the Old Hickory company
in its 1931 catalogue, this couch offers meticulously
wrapped arms and excessive spindles. It brings a
feeling of high style within the rustic setting.

The Fisherman's Cabin at Manka's Inverness Lodge in Inverness, California, is the setting for this scene. The cabin is complete with a high-end collection of hickory furniture and antique rustic accessories. Louie, the dog, can be rented with any room at the inn! The chairs and footstool were made by prison inmates in Putnamville, Indiana, between 1929 and the early 1980s.

Above: A high-end set of hickory furniture consists of this rare end table, rocker and table lamp with antique mica shade.

Above right: This short-arm chair with casters functions as a desk chair. Such chairs are upholstered in a variety of fabrics.

Above: This magnificent glider rests on the porch of a contemporary trapper's cabin in the mountains of Montana. Just a few steps from a great trout pond, the owners often sit here to rig their fishing gear.

Right: This pair of large armchairs first appeared on the market around 1920, and in 1929 they were offered for sale at the high price of $15 each.

Facing: Arguably my all-time favorite porch, this setting is located at Manka's Inverness Lodge in Inverness, California. Besides the paddle-arm chairs made by Old Hickory, the porch also offers a hot tub big enough for two.

This 1920s Rustic Hickory Furniture Company table served as my computer desk for many years. Now my six-year-old daughter uses it for her homework and her never-ending collection of dolls.

Below: A set of Old Hickory Windsor armchairs surrounds a dramatic root dining table.

This three-drawer chest with detached mirror was made by the Indiana Willow Products Furniture Company. The clean lines and simple form make these items compatible in any setting.

This Old Hickory bureau made in the 1920s is constructed of oak dimensional wood and hickory saplings. Few such pieces exist, as when they were first offered they retailed at $55—a large amount at the time.

A very tall bed made by the Bedford Hickory Furniture Company in the 1930s. The owner of the company, Luther A. Simons, also owned two other hickory companies that were located in the towns of Columbus and Colfax, Indiana. Many pieces of furniture from these companies were placed in hundreds of motels throughout the country.

Below: This set of bunk beds was created by the Indiana Willow Products Company in the mid-1940s. They grace a gorgeous lakeside home in upstate Maine. An original Gustav Stickley bureau rests in the corner of the room.

This early Old Hickory desk
was found on a porch in
New Hampshire years ago.
Today it serves as my
daughter's computer desk.

IDENTIFYING AND DATING HICKORY FURNITURE

There are several misconceptions regarding hickory furniture that should be clarified and corrected. As time has passed, it seems that all hickory furniture is commonly referred to as Old Hickory. Much the same way as *refrigerator* and *xerox* have become common names that originally were brand names, the adoring public mistakenly calls anything with bark on it Old Hickory. The most obvious misuse of the term is apparent on eBay, the online auction service. Under the title "Old Hickory" you'll find items such as souvenir wood (made from ash), Gypsy furniture (made of willow) and all kinds of other items created from bark-on branches commonly and mistakenly referred to as Old Hickory. So in a meager attempt to set the record straight, here are some guidelines for both identifying and dating hickory furniture.

For history buffs interested in an extended lesson and documentation on the history of the Indiana hickory furniture movement, please refer to my book *History of the Old Hickory Chair Company and the Indiana Hickory Furniture Movement*, 1995, 2002. However, here are a few pointers that will aid in an understanding of the effort.

There were at least ten different companies manufacturing hickory furniture in Indiana. The largest was the Old Hickory Chair Company in Martinsville. With the exception of very few pieces, if it is not signed "Old Hickory," then the Old Hickory company did not make it. Keep in mind that the Jasper Hickory Furniture Company in Jasper, Indiana, just took the Old Hickory Furniture Company catalogue and copied every last piece in their own factory. Their pieces, generally, were never signed. So for the collector, if Old Hickory is what you want, be sure the piece is stamped with the Old Hickory mark. While it's true

A traditional "brand" by Old Hickory. Such signatures can be found on chair backs, table legs and the undersides of tabletops. If the brand reads "Old Hickory Chair Company," the piece was made before 1922. If it reads "Old Hickory Furniture Company," it was made in 1922 and beyond.

that the Old Hickory Chair Company produced a very limited amount of high-end designer pieces in the very early part of the twentieth century that were unsigned, such pieces almost never appear or come on the market.

Further, the Old Hickory Chair Company changed their name to the Old Hickory Furniture Company in

1921. Almost all of the Old Hickory pieces were branded, usually on table bottoms or chair legs. The brands read several different ways throughout the years of the company, including:

OLD HICKORY CHAIR COMPANY,

MARTINSVILLE, INDIANA

OLD HICKORY FURNITURE COMPANY,

MARTINSVILLE, IND.

OLD HICKORY, MARTINSVILLE, INDIANA.

They also often—especially in their early years (1890s–1920s) and then in later years (1940s–1970s)—affixed a paper label. Sometimes round and sometimes square, the labels read "Old Hickory" and included other information as well. In the 1930s, they started using a round, dime-size copper tag that read "Genuine Old Hickory, Bruce Preserved, Martinsville, Indiana." (The 1941 Old Hickory catalogue tag read "Chemically Preserved" instead of "Bruce Preserved.") There is always a number in the center of the tag. That number is the year the piece was made. *Bruce Preserved* refers to a process they used that included insecticides and varnishes. The dime-size tag is referred to as a "Bruce Tag."

There are other ways to date hickory furniture as well. The material used to weave the seats and backs evolved throughout the history of the hickory furniture movement. Initially, beginning in the 1890s, strips of inner-bark hickory shaved from hickory trees was used as seating material. Up until the 1930s, the Old Hickory company used a herringbone pattern to weave the hickory strips in their seats and chair backs. The 1931 catalogue from Old Hickory shows for the first time the quarter-round outer layer of the rattan plant on a few of their products. That same year was also the first year that wood slatted seats appeared in the Old Hickory catalogue. Further, 1941 was the first year that an open weave (also called porch weave) was pictured in the Old Hickory catalogue.

Keep in mind that there were other influential hickory manufacturers at this time. One was the Columbus Hickory Furniture Company, of Columbus, Indiana. In the late 1930s, rattan—the material used for weaving seats and backs and imported from both Japan and Germany—was difficult to obtain. Luther A. Simons, the owner of the Columbus company (and other hickory furniture companies as well), created a product called Simonite. It was a soft, pliable, thick paper weave made from the by-products of spruce trees. Many hickory chairs and beds were woven from this material. It is still in use today.

At the same time, wooden slats appeared on hickory chairs from several different companies. Further, Old Hickory and other companies from the mid-1930s often wove seat chairs and backs from wide strips of canvas or nylon. These were then covered with upholstered cushions. In the 1930s, the inner layer of the rattan plant was used as weaving material by many of the hickory manufacturing companies. Old Hickory referred to this material as "flat reed."

Throughout the rest of the Old Hickory period, weaving patterns included herringbone, open weave and a combination of other patterns. Some pieces have been found that combine both hickory strips and rattan as the weaving material. The company also began using strips of hickory again in the 1940s.

Another few comments are in order. Old Hickory never, ever made salesmen's samples. Salesmen traveled with catalogues and a full-size example of their firm's work. Old Hickory toys, first appearing in the 1901 catalogue and finally in the 1914 catalogue, are frequently mistaken as salesmen's samples. Old Hickory sold their toys in a cardboard box that contained two chairs, a settee and a table. Further, painted Old Hickory furniture first appeared in the 1922 catalogue. Colors included green, blue, white and brown.

A traditional herringbone pattern.

A standard straight weave incorporating both rattan and hickory strips.

A traditional "open" or "porch weave" pattern.

BIBLIOGRAPHY

Alexander, Jennie. Letter to author, 7 May 1994.

"Articles of Incorporation, State of Indiana," Indiana Willow Products Company, 27 February 1937.

"Articles of Incorporation, State of Indiana," Jasper Hickory Furniture Company. 21 October 1929.

"Articles of Incorporation, State of Indiana." Hoosier Hickory Manufacturing Company, 31 December 1926.

Bedford (IN) Telephone Directory, September 1941, 1943 and 1949.

"Bob Schnaus Played Leading Role in Jasper," *Jasper (IN) Herald* 8 February 1994.

"Brief Sketches of Jasper Wood Plants," *Jasper (IN) Daily Herald*, 20 July 1966.

Brown, Lib. "Last of the Old Hickory Furniture Company . . ." *Martinsville (IN) Reporter*, 12-8-1978.

Bruns, Alice. Interview by author. Martinsville, Indiana, June 1994.

"Building Addition to Colfax Furniture Factory," *Clinton County (IN) Review*, 5 July 1928.

"Business History, Morgan Co.," *Times*, 28 November 1984.

"Certificate of Incorporation, State of Indiana," Rustic Hickory Furniture Company, 2 January 1903.

"Chair Factory Locating Here," *Clinton County (IN) Review*, 22 September 1927.

"Chicago Paper Features Old Hickory Exhibit," *Business and Industry Furniture Factory*, 7 January 1938.

"City Acquiring New Factory for Opening on February 15," *The Bedford (IN) Times*, 6 January 1941.

"Colfax History," *Colfax (IN) Centennial*, 1948.

"Contract Let for Addition to Chair Factory," *Clinton County (IN) Review*, 31 May 1928.

"Corporation Board of Director Minutes, 9-26-1900." Morgan Co. Historical Archives, Book 3.

Cottingham, Mike, and Helen Cottingham. Interviewed by author. Jasper, Wyoming, 15 June 1994.

Cottingham, Helen. Letter to author, 27 June 1994 and 24 July 1994.

Couch, Joanne. "Old Hickory Has Barrel of Fun Making Furniture," *Tribune and Star Courier*, 17 August 1969.

De Valle, D., Norberg, D. "Charles Limbert, Maker of Michigan Arts and Crafts Furniture," *Herald*, Henry Ford Museum, October 1976.

Derringer, Wilbur. Telephone interview by author, 27 July 1994.

Fierst, John. Letter to author, 25 July 1994.

"Fire at Furniture Factory," *Clinton County (IN) Review*, 4 October 1928.

"Fire Destroys Part of Factory," *Martinsville (IN) Recorder*, 9 July 1968.

"Fire Wrecks Rustic Factory," *Laporte (IN) Argus*, 20 April 1903.

Fletcher, Dorothy. Interview by author. Martinsville, Indiana, June 1994.

"Furniture Factory Will Be Largest Kind in World," *Bedford (IN) Mail*, 6 January 1941.

Garron, Christian G. *Limbert Arts and Crafts Furniture, The Complete 1905 Catalogue*. New York: Dover Publications, 1992.

Gilborn, Craig. "Adirondack Hickory Furniture," *Art and Antiques*, January 1981.

Gilborn, Craig. *Adirondack Furniture*. New York, New York: Abrams, 1987.

Gray, Leon. "Finding Mineral Water Here Was an Accident," *Martinsville (IN) Reporter*, 12 April 1976.

Gutherie, James, M. "A Quarter Century In Lawrence County, Indiana 1917–1941," Bedford, Indiana, 1984.

Handley, Ken. Interview by author, 20 April 1993.

Letter to author, 6 February 1989.

Hines, Hugh. Interviewed by Kathryn Boyce, Martinsville, Indiana, 13 March 1973.

"History of Laporte County," A Twentieth Century History. 1977.

"History of Laporte County," n.d., n.p.

Huxley, Francis. Letter to author, 24 April 1994.

Indiana Hickory Furniture Company Advertisement. *Altrix*, 1928.

"J. & S. Hickory Mfg. Co. Are Now Turning Out Chairs," *Clinton County (IN) Review*, 22 December 1927.

Johnson, Maxine. Interview by author. Oolitic, Indiana. May 1994.

Kerr, Ann. *The Collectors Encyclopedia of Russel Wright*. Paducah, Kentucky: Collector Books, 1990.

Kylloe, Ralph. "A Guide to Rustic Furniture," *Log Home Illustrated*, March 1994: 1021.

Kylloe, Ralph. "Further Perspectives On Rustic Designs." *Arts and Crafts Quarterly 7*, no. 2 (1994): 3031.

Kylloe, Ralph. "Indiana Hickory Furniture, an Aire of Definite Sincerity," *Traces, A Publication of the Indiana Historical Society*. Winter (1994): 4447.

Kylloe, Ralph. "Rush For Rustic," *Arts and Crafts Conference Catalogue*, 1990: 5861.

Kylloe, Ralph. "Rustic Furniture Brought Nature Indoors," *Antique Week*, Knightstown, Indiana (1988): 12.

Kylloe, Ralph. "Rustic Revival: Indiana Old Hickory," *Arts and Crafts Quarterly 2*, no. 2 (1988): 1820.

Kylloe, Ralph. "The Rise of Rustic." *Log Home Living*, May (1994): 7582.

Kylloe, Ralph. *Indiana Hickory Furniture*. Londonderry, New Hampshire: Rustic Publications, 1988.

Kylloe, Ralph. *Rustic Furniture Makers*. Gibbs Smith, Publisher, 1995.

Kylloe, Ralph. *Rustic Furniture*. Museum of Our National Heritage, July 1989.

Kylloe, Ralph. *Rustic Traditions*. Layton, Utah: Gibbs Smith, Publisher, 1993.

Kylloe, Ralph. *The Collected Works of Indiana Hickory Furniture Makers*. Londonderry, New Hampshire: Rustic Publications, 1989.

"Laporte Factory Crippled by Fire," *Laporte (IN) Daily Herald*, 20 April 1903.

Laughner, Emerson. Approximately ten interviews were conducted by author between 1987 and 1993.

Lory, Erma. Interview by author. Nashville, Indiana, July 1994 and May 1993.

Martin, H. H. Laporte, *Indiana History of First Hundred Years*. Laporte, Indiana, 1932.

"Martinsville, Indiana Pluck and Toil," *Business and Industry*, 1949.

McMcary, Ruth. Letters to author, 4 May and 16 May 1994.

McMillon, Bill. *The Old Hotels and Lodges of Our National Parks*. South Bend, Indiana: Icarus Press, 1983.

"Miles Bros. Hope For Higher Quality Growth," *Martinsville (IN) Reporter*, 23 January 1970.

Miller, Xenia. Three interviews by author. One in person and two by phone, 1987 and 5 May 1994.

Mitchel, Charles. Two interviews by author, 1987 and 1 July 1994.

"Native Business Interests Of Martinsville," *Martinsville (IN) Republican*, Industrial Edition, 1898.

"New Industry Aids Life to City," *Vincennes (IN) Sun*, 20 May 1934.

"Newspaper Advertisements for Rustic Hickory Dealers," Rustic Hickory Furniture Company, Laporte, Indiana, ca 1925.

Nunn, Bette. "Old Hickory Chair Co. Organized in 1898," *Martinsville Reporter*, n.d.

"Old Hickory A-Go-Go' Declares New Management," *Martinsville (IN) Reporter*, 23 December 1965.

"Old Hickory Buy Barrel Equipment," *Martinsville (IN) Daily Reporter*, 9 November 1970.

"Old Hickory Chair Company," Company catalogue, 1912.

"Old Hickory Chair Company," Company catalogue, Martinsville, Indiana, 1910.

"Old Hickory Chair Company," Martinsville (IN) Reporter, 131989.

"Old Hickory Closing Makes More Unemployed," Martinsville (IN) Reporter, 8 July 1978.

"Old Hickory Furniture Company," Company catalogue, 1931.

"Old Hickory Furniture Company," Company catalogue, 1937.

"Old Hickory Furniture Company," Company catalogue, 1942.

"Old Hickory Furniture Company," Company catalogue, 1957.

"Old Hickory Has Changed Name," 8 February 1921.

"Old Hickory–Circa 1898," Morgan County Scrapbook, Vol. 1., n.d.

Osborn, Susan. American Rustic Furniture. New York, New York: Harmony Books, 1984.

Patton, McGuiness, Mrs. Interview by author. Martinsville, Indiana, July 1994.

"Price list and Index of Rustic Hickory Furniture," Rustic Hickory Furniture Company, 1934.

"Quisisana to Erect New Factory Building," Laporte (IN) Daily Herald, 3 October 1903.

"Ramada Inn Merges with Old Hickory," Martinsville (IN) Reporter, 10 December 1968.

"Rustic Hickory Corporation," Laporte, Indiana Supplement B. Circa 1930.

"Rustic Hickory Furniture Company," Company catalogue, 1913.

"Rustic Hickory Furniture Company," Company catalogue, Laporte, Indiana. 1934.

"Rustic Hickory Furniture Company," Company catalogue, Laporte, Indiana. 1915.

"Rustic Hickory Furniture Company," Laporte (IN) Argus, 1905.

"Rustic Hickory Furniture," n.p., n.d.

Schnaus, Edward, Urban, O.S.B. Letter to Author, 26 April 1994 and 12 May 1994.

Schnaus, Robert, F. Reminiscences. 5 May 1932.

Schnaus-Smith, Ruth. Letter to author, 27 June 1994.

"Several Pieces of Old Hickory Furniture. . . ." Clinton County (IN) Review, 16 February 1928.

"Shircliff Industries, Inc., Open New Furniture Factory in Vincennes," Vincennes (IN) Post, 4 June 1935.

"Small Blaze at Chair Factory," Clinton County (IN) Review, 25 Oct 1928.

Snider, Harold. Interview by author. Morgantown, Indiana, May 1994.

Spangle, Brian. Letter to author, 11 April 1994.

Stephenson, Sue. Rustic Furniture. New York, New York: Van Nostrand Reinhold, 1979.

Stickley, Gustav. Craftsman Homes. New York, New York: Craftsman Publishing Company, 1909.

Storm, Ralph. History of Martinsville. WPA Publication, 1936.

Terra Haute City Directory, 1927 and 1929.

"The Old Hickory," Martinsville (IN) Republican, n.d.

Toms, Tubby. "Factory Omitted in Hickory List," n.d., n.p.

U.S. Department of Agriculture. Wood Handbook: Wood as an Engineering Material. Washington, D.C.: U. S. Department of Agriculture, 1974.

Vincennes City Directory, 1937 and 1939.

Walls, Bette. "Old Hickory Co. Holds Memories for Many Folk," n.d., n.p.

Wheaton, Rodd. "Rustic Connotations: Furnishing National Park Hostelries" (1975).

Wood, Mickey. Letter to author, 15 February 1994 and 1 March 1994.

"Work on New Factory Progressing Rapidly," Clinton County (IN) Review, 27 October 1927.

SOURCES FOR RUSTIC FURNISHINGS

Appalachian Rustic Furniture
33 North Dade Park Drive
Wildwood, GA 30757
1.866.5hickory
www.arfurniture.com

Flat Creek Rustic Furniture
Jerry Sluder
173 Old Mars Hill Highway
Weaverville, NC 28787
828.645.5899
www.flatcreekrustics.com

Flat Rock Furniture, Inc.
215 E. Pullman Street
PO Box 65
Waldron, IN 46182
765.525.5265
www.flatrockfurniture.net

Hickory Furniture Designs, Inc.
Brad McQueen
107 W. 14th Street
Lapel, IN 46051
765.534.4243
Fax: 765.534.4246
www.hickoryfurnituredesigns.com

Old Hickory Furniture Company
403 South Noble Street
Shelbyville, IN 46176
317.392.6740
www.oldhickory.com

Ralph Kylloe
Ralph Kylloe Gallery
PO Box 669
Lake George, NY 12845
518.696.4100
www.ralphkylloe.com <http://www.ralphkylloe.com/>
info@ralphkylloe.com

For free appraisals and information on the history or mainte-
nance of hickory furniture.

Woods Rustic Furnishings
1013 Washington Avenue
Shelbyville, IN 46176
317.392.4347

Yesterday's Furniture
RR1 Box 92
Bloomfield, IN 47424
812.876.0493
www.rustichickoryfurniture.com